Queen of To-morrow

The Princess's smile

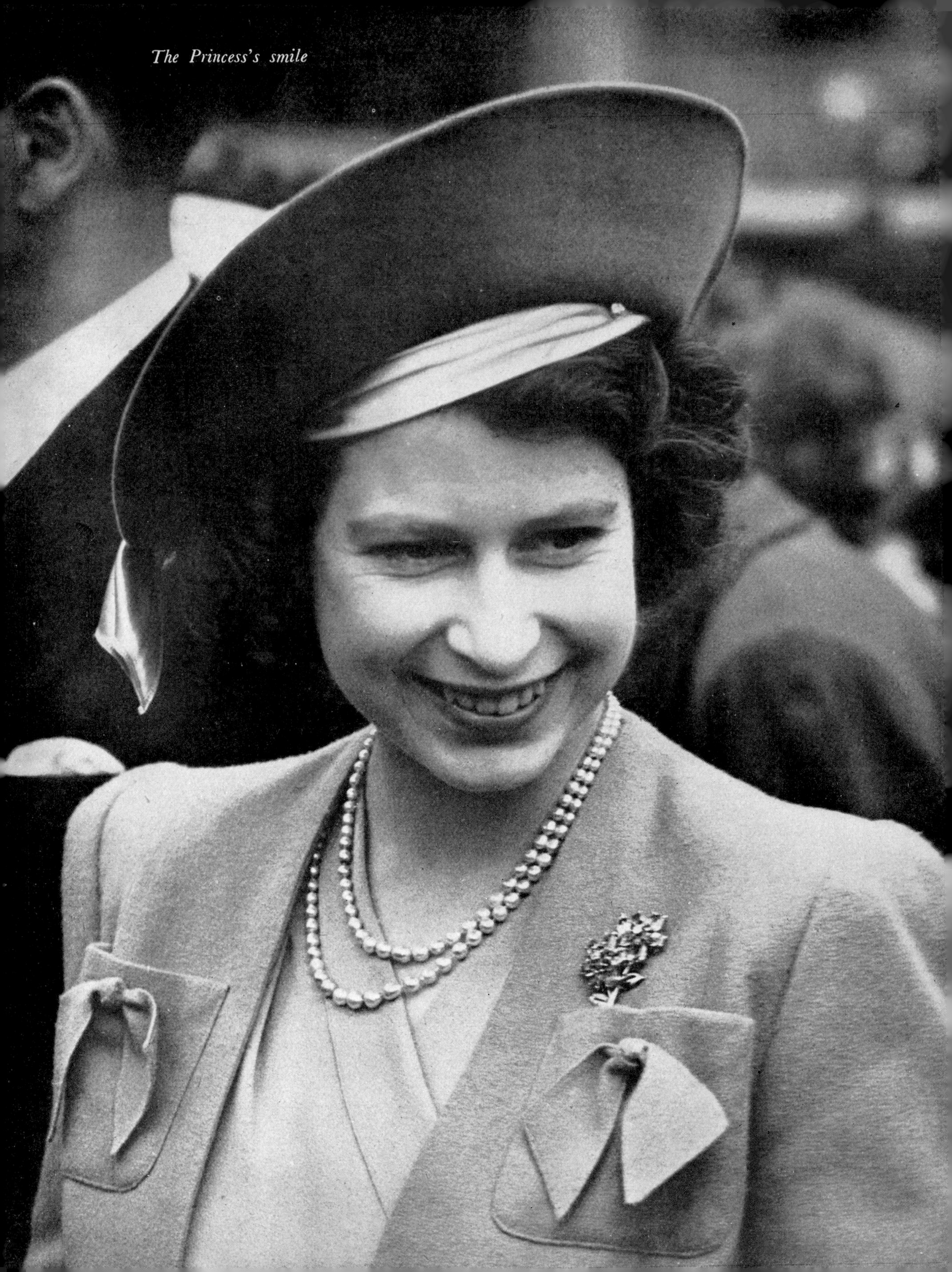

Queen of To-morrow

An Authentic Study of
H.R.H. The Princess Elizabeth

By

Louis Wulff M.V.O.

Part author
" The Royal Family in Wartime "

London
Sampson Low, Marston & Company, Limited

Acknowledgment is made for the black and white illustrations in this book to the following :—

Mr. Graham Thompson of the Newsreel Association of Great Britain and Ireland Ltd.

The Photographic News Agencies Ltd.

Fox Photos Ltd.

Planet News Ltd.

New York Times Photos—London.

The Times.

The Daily Graphic.

London News Agency Photos, Ltd.

The Associated Press Ltd.

Ministry of Information. Crown Copyright Reserved.

Central Press Photos Ltd.

Keystone Press Agency Ltd.

Portrait by Dorothy Wilding.

The Topical Press.

Marcus Adams.

Studio Lisa.

P.A.—Reuter Photos.

Made and Printed in Great Britain by Purnell and Sons Limited
Paulton (Somerset) and London

AUTHOR'S FOREWORD

It is with some deliberateness that I have chosen the title of this book, the first attempt to portray something of the personality, character and charm of Princess Elizabeth since she has grown up.

Apart from her constitutional position as Heiress Presumptive to the Throne, which means that one day—may it be long distant!—she will, in the natural course of events, be called upon to reign as the next Sovereign of the Royal House of Windsor, she is Queen of To-Morrow in another sense as well. Not only is she the living embodiment of the future hopes and aspirations of the great British Commonwealth of Nations, but, as she approaches her twenty-first birthday, and enters on full womanhood, she is the representative-in-chief of the new generation, the heritors of the post-war world, the young men and women whose lot it may well be to witness the unfolding of the Atomic Age; whose lives we pray will be lived out in the era of world peace which to-morrow may bring.

L.W.

East Horsley,
  Surrey.
May, 1946.

A day at the races with the King

CONTENTS

Godmother and Baby Elizabeth Lavinia Sara King

CHAPTER ONE

The Personality of a Princess

WRITING at the time of the Silver Jubilee of King George V, when three quarters of the world was still believing in permanent peace, while the other quarter was preparing secretly and wilfully for war, John Drinkwater picked out as the most noticeable feature of the King's twenty-five years reign the fact that the British monarchy, in spite of a war which had shaken civilisation, in spite of the challenge to class distinctions thrown out by the surge of the new democracy, had emerged after a period of unprecedented change in the organisation of human society, to stand higher than ever in public affection and international prestige.

Since then another more dreadful war has almost shattered civilisation. Human society has known strange and awful changes. Evil new conceptions of government and state have risen, and been crushed, perhaps to leave some tiny contribution towards the ultimate good of humanity amid the welter of their ruin; and the shadow of the atomic bomb presages a future world so different that no man may guess at its form or know whether from the split nucleus of the uranium atom is to come freedom and leisure for all mankind, or the final doom and extinction of the human race. But through all, the British monarchy has stood firm, as it did before. The reverberations of the atom bombs that fell on Hiroshima and Nagasaki have shaken many things, but not the solid foundations of the British throne. The ideals of the British commonwealth of nations, the love of freedom, the hatred of oppression, the desire to live and work in peace that Britain and her sister nations of the Empire share so completely, are to-day more than ever before the common ideals of all men, the basis of hope for a world brotherhood of all nations. And since it is nothing but the narrow gold circlet of the Imperial Crown that binds together Britain and her grown-up independent Dominions in their free, family association, it is natural that other countries should evince a deep and abiding interest in the workings of our monarchial system, and in the personality of the wearer of that twenty-inch circle of gold that spans the world. In turn, the wearer of that Crown has, as head of the British Empire, a special responsibility to the world at large such as does not fall to any other head of State. The Empire which he guides, and over whose destinies he must preside, is the first practical, working example of a free international brotherhood of equal nations, each enjoying its own sovereignty, yet each owing equal allegiance to the same Sovereign. It must be his dread responsibility, as it can be that of no other living soul, to see that nothing is allowed to impede its successful development, to smooth away all internal differences or difficulties that may threaten to halt its majestic progress.

To-day, fate has placed the future destinies of the Imperial Crown into the slender hands of a girl of twenty, Her Royal Highness the Princess Elizabeth, Heiress Presumptive to the British Throne.

Princess Elizabeth Alexandra Mary Windsor, who was born in a private house at No. 17 Bruton Street, London, W., a few yards away from the busy traffic of Bond Street,

*At the East End of London on a drive with the King and Queen after VE day. There were no barriers
between the crowds and the Royal family.*

at twenty minutes to three in the morning of Wednesday, April 21, 1926, is thus destined
to a life apart, is consecrated to the service of her father's people whose Queen she will
one day be, and, in a wider sense, to the service of all mankind. How she fulfils her
duties to-day, the indications of what kind of a Queen she may be to-morrow, are matters
of great import, meriting the attention of the statesmen of the world, and arousing the
interest of thoughtful men and women everywhere. For though the executive powers
of the Crown have shrunk and diminished with the passing centuries and the widening
of democracy, its power and influence by guidance and example have steadily grown
as the Press, the cinema, and most of all, the radio, have established closer, more personal
contact between King and people, until to-day they stand higher and reach out to wider,
vaster fields than ever. So on what manner of person wears the Crown as much depends
as ever. Not only by official acts, but by the mode of his own private life, the Sovereign
of to-day exercises a power that may not always be realised, but is very real, a position
which involves necessarily a great sacrifice of his personal freedom.

Princess Elizabeth's future is, so far as human mind may foresee, mapped out inexorably
for her. It is not by her choice of a way of life, but by the manner in which she carries
out the great duties and fulfils the high obligations laid on her, that she can achieve
success or meet failure. And every indication of her life so far points to resounding
success.

A Princess who is heiress to her father's throne has great privileges and many advantages.
But there are restrictions and limitations to offset and balance them. Whatever high
prerogatives may be hers, she can never enjoy the right to lead a normal, private life, that

is shared by all her father's subjects, high and low, in each and all of his Dominions. Wherever she goes, whatever she does, she must be followed by the searchlight of publicity, and she can be free only within certain very narrow limits to plan and shape her own life. That is part, and no small part, of the burden of kingship, especially of modern kingship. In the eyes of a young girl that burden must loom most heavily. The thought of this inheritance of self-abnegation to which he was automatically committing certainly his elder, and perhaps as well his younger, daughter, is said to have been one of the considerations that weighed most deeply on the King when he was called on to decide his own future at the time of the abdication of his brother, Edward VIII. Whether the Duke of York, as he then was, was free to refuse the crown whose weight his brother had found so great that he had fain to put it down, is a point on which no definite light has been thrown: but the finger of duty pointed only one way. The Duke had been trained both as a young Prince, and as a naval officer, to know his duty and to do it without regard for his personal feelings, and he could allow no personal feelings, however deep, to stop him now. But the thought of the two young Princesses, then aged ten and a half and six years respectively, whose duty he must do for them, and who could not themselves know anything of the changes, immediate and immense, brought into their lives in consequence of their father's act, cannot have failed to give him pause.

In the years that have passed since that day of history, December 11, 1936, Princess Elizabeth has become, more and more, a world figure.

Now, at the threshold of her twenty-first year, she is one of the most popular girls in the world, a centre of interest throughout the British Isles, the Dominions, the colonies,

In a semi-state landau she drives with the Royal party to St. Paul's for the VE Thanksgiving Service.

and in the United States. More space is devoted to her in the newspapers of the world, week by week, more photographs appear of her, than of anyone else of her age in the world. But the world, as yet, knows very little about her. Those who have seen her are numbered in thousands, those who want to see her in millions. Something of the ancient magic of kingship clings to her, drawing men and women from their work and their homes, ten miles and more across country, to catch a fleeting glimpse of her as she passes in a car, packing the streets wherever she goes, focusing on her activities, her personality and her character an interest that is world-wide.

What kind of a girl is she?

Thanks to the happy family atmosphere which has always surrounded her, thanks to the care with which her mother and father guarded and shielded her in her early years from publicity and officialdom alike, she has grown up unspoilt, natural, and charming.

The Princess in the City : at London's Mansion House with the Lord Mayor.

From the day of her father's accession, the course of her life had to change in impetus if not in direction. Her training and education, which had always been designed with a view to the possibility that she might eventually succeed to the Throne, were gradually altered so that by degrees she should become aware at a comparatively early age of her position, duties and responsibilities as Heiress-Presumptive. But the King and Queen were determined not to allow either of their daughters to come too early into the public eye, or to make any but the minimum of appearances at functions of an official nature, so that it was not until she was sixteen that Princess Elizabeth took up any activities outside the sphere of her own home and the normal interests and pursuits of an ordinary English girl. As a result, she has a foundation of happiness and stability on which to build her future, and the first thing that impresses nearly everyone meeting her is her naturalness and sincerity.

No matter whom she may meet, the manager of a big factory, a member of her father's Government, a foreign Ambassador, a girl at a work-bench, a green-jerseyed Land Girl to whom she has just given a long service badge, a Guardsman in the ranks of a parade she is inspecting, she looks at each with the same steadfast, direct, tranquil gaze, listens to each with the same interested attention, speaks to each in that same softly-rounded, musical voice that is so compellingly reminiscent of her mother. The Princess's voice is, indeed, a happy voice to hear, and you may often see, on the faces of people within earshot who are not themselves talking to her, a smile of pleasure as they listen to her, so much of youth and charm and beauty and happiness are blended in her accents.

Her eyes are blue, but what exact shade of blue is a matter of some question. Half a dozen people after talking to her will hazard half a dozen different opinions. Perhaps the most nearly accurate was the description given by a poetically-minded Irishman who met her in Ulster. "Her eyes are sea blue," he said, and the Princess's large and lustrous eyes do change colour as the sea does sometimes, seeming deep blue, now changing to lighter colour. On occasion, too, her eyes take on a much colder colour, the pale blue of ice, if, as does rarely happen, she finds it necessary to check presumption or intrusion.

She has exquisitely delicate fair colouring, the same complexion of rose and cream which her aunt, the Princess Royal, had as a young girl. This lovely colouring is one of the Princess's great charms, and it is lost in her pictures, even those taken by the latest and most scientific of modern colour process. Her vivacity and animation, which also form an integral part of her attraction, are similarly lost in photographs, so that nearly everyone comments after a first sight of her, "She is so much more attractive than her pictures!"

Her hair, golden and curly when she was a baby, is now a warm shade of darkish brown, glinting with lighter tones. She wears it parted to the side, with three soft rows of curls at the back of the neck. Her teeth are white, large, even-spaced and well-cared for.

Her smile comes more rarely than that of her mother, but has much of that elusive charm that has made the Queen's smile world famous. It illumines her whole face, radiating charm and friendliness, saying more expressively than words that she is happy to be wherever she may be: for it is a characteristic of the heiress to the throne of England that she does not allow her tremendous responsibilities, no matter how seriously she may view them, to spoil her sense of fun or her deep enjoyment of life. She is a happy person, with the gift of making those around her feel happy, too. From her earliest days, she has been fortunate in entire freedom from that shyness, that nervous freezing of the senses which her father and her uncles, and her grandmother, Queen Mary, as well, found a difficult obstacle which had to be surmounted before they could be at ease in public life. By contrast, the Princess always appears at ease. To converse with a foreign visitor of high distinction at a formal reception in the ornate gold and crimson State Rooms of Buckingham Palace is no more effort for her than to talk to a factory girl in overalls and cap bending over a busily working machine. She does both with equal ease and naturalness. So utterly free is she from selfconsciousness, so completely has she the secret of putting others at their ease that on many occasions, working girls and men, after a few moments' talk with her, have felt surprised to realise it was really the Princess to whom they

Playing with dolls is a thing of long ago: but the Princess finds interest in a Russian Court lady in period dress at an exhibition of Dolls of All Nations.

An Indian student from Bombay meets the Princess: an Empire incident at the College of Nursing, Cavendish Square, London.

had been chattering, a feeling which Princess Elizabeth herself would regard as the very highest form of compliment.

Both the distinguished foreigner and the factory hand are likely to agree on another facet of the Princess's character—her quick intelligence. Ambassadors of friendly Powers have, as an integral part of their duties, the charge of keeping their own governments at home well-informed about the leading personalities of the country to which they are accredited, so that there is no need to have broken the seals of any diplomatic "bags" to know that the name of the heiress to the Throne occurs not infrequently in the dispatches sent home to various chanceries from the Ambassadors and Ministers at the Court of St. James's. For this reason, a special importance attaches to conversations between the Princess and the heads and members of missions attached to her father's Court. Discreet and diplomatic as Ambassadors must of necessity be, it is no secret at St. James's that all members of the Corps Diplomatique, however violently they may disagree on other points, are in agreement on this, that Princess Elizabeth is a young woman of much more than average discernment and intelligence, with an excellent background of general knowledge as well as an outstanding grasp of modern history, recent events and trends of thought, that enable her to discuss questions of the day, both

THE PERSONALITY OF A PRINCESS

A "bathing the baby" lesson : a young Red Cross nurse shows the Princess how it should be done, with the aid of a doll model.

domestic and foreign, with anyone. A factor that probably adds much to the general high opinion of the Princess held in ambassadorial circles is that she can speak and express herself with equal ease and clarity on almost any subject in French as well as in her own tongue.

Judging the matter from an entirely different view point, the factory hand arrives at the same conclusion simply because, in the course of a few moments' talk, the Princess so easily grasps the working principles of whatever piece of intricate machinery she is being shown: and reveals a surprising understanding of, and sympathy with, the other's point of view and problems.

Kingship, as we know, has survived in England when in most other countries it has died. But it has changed in character through the centuries, it is still changing to-day. Perhaps that is the secret of its survival, its ability to adapt itself to the changing conditions of a developing world. As the duties of the monarchy have altered, so, in a degree, has the training of its scions.

Already, at twenty, Princess Elizabeth knows many aspects of national life of which her great-great-grandmother, Queen Victoria, never could have had knowledge. She has in no sense been brought up in a glass case. The rarefied air of Courts has not been permitted

15

QUEEN OF TO-MORROW

Statecraft, politics, knowledge of the world and of humanity, all these are the necessary accomplishments of Princes and the groundwork for them has not been omitted from Princess Elizabeth's education. But she was neither forced precociously in a hothouse of Royal learning as a young girl, nor circumscribed in her studies and entertainments when she grew older. As Windsor Castle, for example, she has for several years had the unrestricted freedom of the great library, with liberty to read what she chooses. Such a happy upbringing is a great tribute to the wisdom and spiritual understanding of her parents. It is the foundation stone for the Princess's character and outlook on life, and the result is that to-day she is a healthy, happy young woman, with a vigorous, lively disposition,

With her very first jewellery : the "Nation's Darling" wears her coral necklace.

One of the most delightful pictures of the Princess as a three-year-old. A birthday study.

serious-minded enough when it is a question of public duty, light-hearted, gay and easy-going at other times, with a never-failing zest for life that makes her a delightful, attractive companion in private, as well as a great success in public. She has, in very considerable measure, that indefinable quality of charm. Her delicate colouring, her firm mouth, she inherits from her grandmother Queen Mary. Her methodical mind, her love of books and learning come from her great-great-grandfather, the Prince Consort, her very observant eye and her keen sense of humour from her father, who enjoys a joke much more, and has a much greater sense of fun, than most people, seeing him only on official occasions, would imagine. Her charm is in the direct line of descent from her mother. There is the same look of quick intelligence and lively sympathy in the eyes, the same sincerity in her gaze, and the same infection in her smile.

Eight years old to-day

VE Day : Princess Elizabeth stands back on the balcony of Buckingham Palace while her father and mother acknowledge the cheers, with the Architect of Victory, Mr. Winston Churchill, between them.

You can see the Queen, too, very clearly, in the way Princess Elizabeth acknowledges the greeting of a crowd. Her arm held up a little away from the shoulder, she waves her hand with just the same graceful motion as her mother. Yet there is a subtle difference in the gesture, just as there is in the quality of her charm, which makes you realise at once that the Princess has a character of her own.

She is decidedly not a person to take things for granted or to be content merely to follow in the footsteps of someone else. The public activities of Royalty necessarily tend to fall into a fairly well defined pattern. The public and semi-public utterances of Royalty must, according to the rules of our monarchic democracy, be largely confined to the expression of innocuous opinions. Definite statements of any kind on controversial issues of the day however deeply felt and generally shared, must not be made, since they might be (and, on one well-known occasion, were in fact) interpreted justly or unjustly, as an attempt to influence political thought. The recorded statements of Royal personages, even on informal, but public, occasions such as a factory visit or the tour of a housing estate, are therefore apt to be guarded and restrained, not to say conventional or dull. They do not always give a full indication of what thoughts may be held in private. Sometimes, however, the real character below the surface is revealed unconsciously by a chance word or act.

Buckingham Palace on VE day, May 8, 1945, was the centre of rejoicing for the victorious Empire. Outside, the teeming thousands of Londoners, men and women of nearly every one of the United Nations mingled with them, stood all day long, packed round the Victoria Memorial, cheering and calling for the King. Inside, there was all the atmosphere that marks a great day. High officials of the Household hurried along the red-carpeted corridors, passed through the war-time fireproof doors, on their way to see

THE PERSONALITY OF A PRINCESS

the King. Ladies-in-waiting came in and out, blue-liveried servants hustled about their business, the police stood patiently behind the high iron gates, now locked against the crowds. Up on the first floor, the red, gold-tasselled draperies hung over the central balcony, where, time after time, in response to the chant of the crowds "We want the King, we want the King," the King and Queen appeared to receive the plaudits of victory. With them, Princess Elizabeth and Princess Margaret came out onto the balcony, gazing with interest, not unmingled perhaps with awe, at the vast concourse of cheering men and women stretching below them. Night came, the floodlights were switched on, and still the crowds called for the King. Again and again the King and Queen and their daughters appeared before the people. Just after eleven o'clock, an idea that had been simmering in Princess Elizabeth's mind most of the day took shape. She spoke to her father—the easy affectionate relations that exist between the King and his daughters are one of the happiest features of the Court of George VI—and, a few minutes later, a small party of two inconspicuously dressed girls, with scarves drawn over their heads, and four men, slipped out of the Palace through the Trade Gate, the servants' entrance in Buckingham Palace Road. Within a few seconds, they were absorbed in the crowd. Not many minutes later, two of the escort of four were separated from the party, leaving only two plain clothes police officers to guard the Princesses as they moved slowly through the thickest sections of the merry revellers. Mostly, they were not recognised. When they were, the good natured crowds made way for them, and the police officers had only to ask them not to make a demonstration, "because that is just what the Princesses don't want". It was after midnight when the Princesses got safely back to the Palace. They walked far through the crowds, and another small page of British Royal history had been written, for never before had the two next in succession to the throne roamed freely round in the midst

VJ Day : the Princess has doffed her uniform : she looks affectionately at her parents as they smile and wave to the cheering crowds. Note the bomb-blasted Palace windows behind.

of a celebrating London crowd outside the Palace on a night of national rejoicing. Next night, they went out again, walking this time as far as Charing Cross and Piccadilly and again returning to the Palace without untoward incident.

The real significance of the episode is deeper than a mere fragment of social history. It is an exact illustration of Princess Elizabeth's initiative and her determination to see things for herself, an indication of her independence of mind, her eagerness for experience, and her courage; courage because merely to look down at the tightly packed thousands in the Mall from the height of the Palace balcony or roof is a frightening sight. It seems

The Princess telephones a friend : note her ordinary pen, and the writing paper headed with the Royal Arms.

as if there *can* be room for not one more. To go voluntarily down among the crowds calls for a certain mental resolve from anyone. For a Princess, used always to having roads cleared for her, crowds held respectfully back, the effort was all the greater. But she *wanted* to see what it was like down there, and was prepared to face whatever difficulties there were in the way. In that strong-willed resolve to allow no ordinary obstacles to stand in her way, of which more instances will be given later in these pages, the Princess shows qualities for which Queen Victoria, whom she resembles in this as in some other ways, was conspicuous.

Another example of her interest in what goes on around her occurred not long ago when she was driving back with the Queen from an engagement in Southwark. The Royal car was passing some of London's first pre-fabricated houses when, to the surprise of the chauffeur and of the escorting police, the order came to stop. Out got the Queen and the Princess, to walk up to the door of a house chosen quite at random, and the most surprised housewife in Britain was soon showing them over her small, cosily furnished home. Many such Royal "surprise" visits are, in fact, arranged in advance. Not so this one. Princess Elizabeth, noticing the new houses, called the Queen's attention to them, asked if she could visit one. The Queen did the rest.

Though she resembles Queen Victoria in more ways than one, Princess Elizabeth is not Victorian in her outlook. Nor, on the other hand, is she excessively a modernist. She has too much character to follow fashion for fashion's sake. Her eyebrows, for instance, are never plucked, nor does she use make-up to any degree. A trace of lipstick, a little powder, are all she uses, and she eschews deep coloured nail varnish. On one occasion Princess Elizabeth did wear full make-up, eye-shadow, heavy powder, vivid lipstick and other aids, but that was for an appearance not in public but before the film cameras, when the King, as his daughter approached eighteen, decided that the public demand to know more of the heiress to the throne could no longer be ignored. Arrangements were made for a short film of the Princess's life, including special "shots" of her in her apartments at Windsor Castle. The cameramen went to Windsor suffering not a little from nerves. It was the Princess's first filming, and there was some natural apprehension about how she would take it, especially as it was necessary, if she were to look natural, under the powerful screening lights, that she should allow herself to be made-up by a studio expert who went with the cameramen.

The apprehension and nervousness left the filming crew as soon as they met the Princess. She put them at ease at once, and, to their astonishment, appeared perfectly at ease herself, without any trace of the self-consciousness which mars so many public figures appearing before the cine-cameras for the first time. Whatever they asked her to do, she did, even allowing sound to be used to record her voice for the first time as she telephoned. When they left, the film men described the Princess as an ideal subject. She showed, they said, instinctive camera sense, and her voice with its light, clear tones, recorded excellently.

To many girls, that would have been an ordeal through which they would have come with not quite the same success. To Princess Elizabeth, it was simply a duty that had to be done, and she did it as she has been trained to do all her duties, high and low, as well as she might, a phrase which with her, nearly always means very well indeed.

Another ordeal of a similar kind had faced the Princess five years earlier, when she went to the microphone for the first time.

Adulation and flattery which in olden days could be, and often were, used to disguise or hide defects in personages of Royal rank, cannot so easily be employed to that dubious end in these more public days when the face and figure of royalty are so much more familiar, so much more commonly seen at first hand among the crowds, more remotely, at second hand, but with even more pitiless clarity, on the screen or in the newspaper pictures. In nothing is this emergence to the open, unbiased judgment of the world at large more pronounced than in the diction and delivery of speeches, heard by all the world at the fireside when Royalty broadcasts. Critics and flatterers alike must bow to the opinion of the majority, for all have here the same opportunity of judging for themselves. To say that Princess Elizabeth has an admirable broadcasting voice, that she has an ease of delivery, a natural sense of the right emphasis of word or phrase, is, therefore, to say something that all who have heard her speak already know. Actually, after her first broadcast, made when she was fourteen and a half, even cynically-minded radio experts, inclined to do anything but overrate a new speaker, were unanimous in their praise—and in their surprise, for the broadcast revealed for the first time to the outside world what was already very well known at Court, that the Princess's voice resembles, almost to an uncanny degree, that of her mother. Apart from an engaging youthful freshness which gives the Princess's voice a lighter tone, there is little to mark the difference between the two. Both have the same clear tone, the same confident ease of enunciation, the same rhythmic flow of diction.

The Princess made her radio debut, fittingly enough, in the B.B.C. Children's Hour, but though the vast majority of her unseen audience were children, it was not altogether of childish things, nor, indeed, on a childish occasion that she spoke.

It was to inaugurate the B.B.C.'s new weekly feature in their war-time service to North America, designed specially for the British children who had been evacuated to Canada or the United States, that she came to the microphone, on Sunday October 13, 1940, and almost her first words were of sympathy for the children separated from their homes and families, and of gratitude to the kind people who had welcomed them to their new countries and homes. "My sister Margaret Rose and I feel so much for you, as we know from experience what it means to be away from those we love most of all," said the Princess, giving one of those fleeting glimpses of the Royal family as just an ordinary, happy family, which delight her hearers. At the end of her broadcast, when she had finished the carefully prepared speech which she had learned so well by heart that only an occasional glance at her "script" on the table before her was necessary, the Princess added another family touch all of her own making. Unknown, of course, to the listeners, Princess Margaret was standing behind her sister while she was speaking, with the King and Queen watching nearby in the same room. Immediately she had finished her last solemn words of reminder to her young hearers that it would be for them, the children of to-day, to make the world of to-morrow a better and happier place when peace came, Princess Elizabeth said quickly, "My sister is by my side, and we are both going to say goodnight to you,—come on, Margaret!" A little breathlessly, ten year old Princess Margaret said her first words into the microphone, "Goodnight!" and Elizabeth added, "Goodnight, and good luck to you all." It was the authentic family note, an ending which any professional radio script writer would have been delighted to have thought out—but in fact it was a spontaneous inspiration of the Princess's.

In Britain, in Canada, in America, in South Africa, and in Malta, where the children of the George Cross Island, unable to be evacuated, were helping their parents to write the splendid annals of bravery which won their island its proud distinction, hundreds upon hundreds of thousands of children, British evacuees and their foster cousins whose homes they were sharing, and thousands of their elders as well, heard the Princess, and from all parts, afterwards, came reports of admiration and praise. In the United States, the Royal broadcast was "Page One" news in the morning papers, and critics, at home and abroad, joined the chorus of praise. One went so far as to describe Princess Elizabeth as the "most outstanding child radio personality I have yet heard", and another remarked truthfully that many a hardened public figure, well accustomed to broadcasting, might envy her clearness and the precision of her delivery. All of this gave very great and justifiable pleasure to the King and Queen, and to the Princess, too, for it was her first big public test, and she had scored an undisputed triumph.

With the tremendous importance of broadcasting as the closest, most intimate channel of direct contact between a modern monarch and the people, the fact that the heiress

At the microphone—Princess Elizabeth rehearsing her first broadcast while Princess Margaret looks on.

presumptive has a natural aptitude as a broadcaster is of no little weight. The secret of what the radio experts love to call her "microphone technique" is very simple. It is that she has no technique at all, but is merely her natural self when she is at the microphone—in itself a very difficult feat, as many who have broadcast once or twice have found out for themselves.

That first broadcast was made from Windsor Castle, where the microphone, because of the danger of air raids, was installed in an underground room. But in spite of its great success, in spite of repeated requests from all parts of the Empire, Princess Elizabeth has not made another direct studio broadcast since then, though records of her voice have been heard on more than one occasion, and once or twice lately her public speeches have been broadcast as she made them.

It was when she launched the great battleship *Vanguard* in December 1944, that the listening public had their next chance of hearing the Princess's voice. B.B.C. microphones, carefully installed on the launching platform, picked up her words, carried them faithfully and instantaneously to the recording van, where they were "stored" on the revolving cylinders for the broadcast later that evening. But those who listened in the evening did not hear all the Princess had said. At the most vital moment, there was a blank, and her voice went off the air. No fault of the B.B.C. engineers was this, but a queer outcome of wartime censorship rules. *Vanguard*, the name of the new battleship, was a very "top" secret. Men who had built her in John Brown's shipyard on the Clyde, were sworn to secrecy, referring to her by a number or some non-committal phrase like "the big ship". Even in the Admiralty itself, only senior officers were supposed to know exactly which ship it was that the Princess had gone north to launch. This, of course, was because her name might easily give the German Admiralty valuable hints as to what size and type of ship it was. So when the Princess said, an unwonted tremor of excitement in her voice, "I name this ship *Vanguard*, may God bless her and all who sail in her," the censor had no option but to cut the fifth word out completely—probably the first time on record that a Royal speech has had to be censored.

As a postscript to that story, it may be mentioned that the German wireless announced the ship's name some twenty-four hours later, some time after which the Admiralty decided that the "secret" need be kept no longer, and revealed that the Princess had named her *Vanguard*. In practice, possession of the name was of little if any value to the enemy intelligence, for the whole design of the *Vanguard* had been radically altered since the original proposals for the new class of battleships, of which she is the first, were published before the war.

The next time the Princess spoke purely for broadcast was in January 1945. This time, she spoke in French, to thank the children of Belgium for their gift of Christmas toys to children in Britain, and the records of her brief speech were flown to Brussels to be broadcast there. It was also broadcast by the B.B.C. so that the Princess had the opportunity of hearing her own voice, and people in this country the opportunity of hearing her French accent. It was judged flawless.

This time, Princess Margaret did not join in, even to add a word of thanks of her own, or to say goodnight, though she, too, speaks

A very tense moment : Princess Elizabeth is in the act of naming the great aircraft carrier H.M.S. Eagle whose bows tower above her.

"Welcome aboard, Ma'am!" : the Princess joins H.M.S. Superb for her crossing to Northern Ireland.

excellent and easy French. Till now the real reason for her silence has not been made known. It was at Sandringham, where both the Princesses were spending their Christmas holidays with the King and Queen that Princess Elizabeth made her recording. Princess Margaret was, therefore, close at hand—but she had mumps!

Princess Elizabeth's first full-scale test came when she crossed the sea for the first time alone to visit Northern Ireland in March 1946, shortly before her twentieth birthday. In a four day programme which included two all-night train journeys, a two hundred mile all-day car drive, the launch of a great ship, official luncheons, and receptions, she carried all before her, winning a success that established her in the hearts of Ulster folk for ever, and that augurs as well as anything could for her future. On this tour, the Princess had an opportunity for showing that she is well able to deal with unexpected situations, such as rarely occur in the carefully planned and prepared visits of Royalty. At Enniskillen, a few miles from the Eire border, men of the Royal Ulster Constabulary had prepared a real Irish surprise for her when she came to inspect their depot, taking her behind a wall of peat blocks into a replica of an illicit mountain still, where two fearsome looking ruffians were distilling poteen with a copper condenser. Scarcely had she got out into the sunshine again, or recovered from her astonishment, when a very smart member of the Constabulary saluted, and handed her a box containing a bottle of the highly illegal spirit, innocently labelled "Mountain Dew". Strictly, this gift was a breach of the law, which several of the accompanying party thought might cause the Princess some

27

embarrassment, especially as she had been given no hint or warning of what was to come. But the Princess accepted the gift with a smile, entering right into the spirit of the joke, to the huge satisfaction of the Constabulary and spectators alike, whose Irish sense of fun was delighted at the thought of the guardians of the law making a present of contraband to the King's daughter. The easy, happy way in which the Princess dealt with that little situation endeared her to Irish hearts more than a score of public speeches could have done.

For train journeys, even on fully official occasions like her Ulster visit, the Princess does not use the Royal train. Instead, she travels in a special coach containing two bedrooms and a sitting room, attached to an ordinary night express, or, if it is a day

She greets an Irish joke with a smile : a member of the Royal Ulster Constabulary presents her with a bottle of highly illegal "poteen".

journey, in a reserved ordinary coach. And she pays full fare for herself and for each member of her suit travelling with her, as well as fees for the special coach.

Proposing her health at a luncheon in her honour, at Belfast, the Governor of Northern Ireland, Admiral Earl Granville, described her as "Our beloved, beautiful, and charming young Princess." Earl Granville is Princess Elizabeth's uncle, and avuncular affection may have influenced his choice of words. But they expressed just what everyone who saw her on that tour, and a great many people who have seen her since, thought and feel about her.

CHAPTER TWO

The Training of a Twentieth Century Princess

PRINCESS ELIZABETH'S training for the duties of Royalty began soon after she had learned to walk. Those first lessons were simple, intended to emphasise, almost unconsciously, with the utmost gentleness, the need for that extra courtesy, that little added touch of consideration for others that has come to be the first social duty of the British Royal family, something we are apt to take as much for granted as we do the courtesy of our police: but something which, again like police courtesy, does not always prevail in other countries.

Since then, her training has gone on with gradually increasing seriousness of purpose, has become more and more complex, wider in its scope, deeper in its implications, to fit her for the vastly complex and deeply significant part she is called on to play in world affairs. An apt and ready pupil in all manner of studies, as ready to learn from books as to gain knowledge from personal experience, the Princess has profited well from her training, until to-day, at the threshold of her life of public service, she is as well and thoroughly equipped for the future as any one may be. It was in the homely atmosphere of her nursery at Piccadilly, at her mother's knee, that the foundations of her great promise to-day were laid, as she learned in simple fashion from perhaps the most charming tutor in the land, the elementary lessons of obedience to God, response to duty, and thoughtfulness for others without which manners, however polished, and wits, however keen, are of little worth. It was from her mother, too, that the Princess learned the first great accomplishment of all, the lessons that are the corner stone of all learning: for it was the Queen who taught her daughter to read.

As she sees and rejoices in the success which the Princess everywhere attains to-day, the Queen may well feel a wholly justifiable pride in the results of her early training. Between the King and Queen and their daughters there exists as complete a mutual relationship of love, trust, understanding and sympathy as could be found throughout the King's dominions, a close-knit family affection that has its deep roots in those nursery days in Piccadilly, where first Elizabeth, then Margaret, were taught, by example and precept, the simple rules of family happiness. Probably at no time ever in the long story of the British monarchy has there existed such a perfect affection and understanding between the Sovereign and the heir to his throne. That particular relationship is agreed by all historians and philosophers to be one of unusual difficulty, calling for the exercise of the greatest tact and delicacy of feeling on either side, and there is no Royal House, including our own, whose record has not been marred by unseemly differences between the reigning monarch of the day and his next-in-succession. Queen Victoria's own early days on the throne were clouded in the reverse direction by antagonism with her mother: much later in her life, her inability to delegate authority to the eldest son with whom she never could manage to see eye to eye, helped to bring misunderstanding and unhappiness to both. Even in much more recent times, in the reign of King George V, the relationship between the King and Queen and the young Princes and their sister was much more formalised than was generally, perhaps, realised at the time outside the immediate Court circle. King George, for example, maintained it as a rule that his sons, when they were living at Buckingham Palace as young men, should always ask permission before coming to see him in his own apartments. Permission was, it is true, rarely, if ever, refused, but the fact remained that his sons and daughter did not have easy open access to their father at all times, which must inevitably have resulted in lessening their mutual understanding. There was a distance between the King and his subjects, which even his own children could not entirely bridge, affectionate and dear as was his regard for each and all of them. Across that little distance, family familiarity was apt sometimes to remain a little strained. Princess Elizabeth and, for the last six years of his life, Princess Margaret, were exempt from this rather austere treatment. Between them and "Grandpa King" there were no barriers. So much did King George delight in the society of his granddaughter that when he was lying at Craigweil House, near Bognor Regis, weak and exhausted after his long fight for life at the end of 1928, Lord Dawson of Penn (who died in 1945) and Sir Stanley Hewett, his two doctors in residence, advised that Princess Elizabeth, then nearly three, should be sent for to raise the King's languid spirits. Happy at her unexpected visit to the seaside, the little Princess played gaily with bucket and spade on the sand in front of her grandfather, while the doctors watched the effect of their new remedy for the depression of long convalescence. They had made a wise decision. The artless remarks of "Lillabet", as the Princess had by that time re-christened herself in her first attempts to pronounce her name, about what she was doing and what she intended to do, brought smiles to the invalid's cheeks, and it is a strange but vouched-for fact that a definite improvement in the King's general condition and spirits at once began to make itself evident. The doctor's remedy came not from the British Pharmacopoeia but from Lord Dawson's wide and deep knowledge of human nature—and it worked.

Between Princess Elizabeth and her mother and father no barriers of State or formality have ever existed. There were none in their Piccadilly home as Duke and Duchess of York, nor at Royal Lodge, the small country house which King George gave them near Windsor Castle: and none was permitted to develop after the accession.

King George VI, his consort, the Heiress to the Throne and her younger sister are, in their private lives, a normal, happily united, English family. The crown, sceptre and orb which, in the Coronation Service at Westminster, set the King apart from the people, have never been allowed to set him

Reverently and gracefully, the khaki-clad Princess places her first wreath at the foot of the Cenotaph beside that of her father.

With the Cabinet and Mr. Churchill watching, she lays her first wreath at the Cenotaph, Armistice Day 1945 apart from his family. That has been Princess Elizabeth's supreme advantage. Heiress to the Throne, she has been able, to a greater extent than any of her predecessors, to enjoy the freedom of family life, to grow up a normal human being, with her personality entirely unspoilt by the fetters of State.

When Princess Elizabeth, daughter of Henry VIII, was a young woman of twenty in 1553, and her sister, Mary, came to the throne, she had to plead ignorance of the Catholic faith to excuse herself from attending Mass. Soon after, she was banished from her sister's Court, and later still, condemned to the Tower as a traitress. Till her sister's death and her own accession, her life was constantly in danger, her most innocent moves watched by Mary's spies, who did not scruple to twist them, whenever they could, into hints of treasonable activity.

Compare that tortuous life of suspicion with the free life of the Princess Elizabeth of our own day, and you have in essence the difference between the despotic autocracy of Tudor days and the leadership-by-example of the constitutional monarchy of Britain to-day.

Princesses, however enlightened and fond of their parents, cannot escape from all the penalties attaching to, and balancing the splendid advantages of, their exalted station. This was a lesson that Princess Elizabeth had to learn before she could talk, long before she had any conception that she was a princess.

It was less than nine months after her birth that the Duke and Duchess of York were compelled to say goodbye to their daughter, and leave her behind in the care of her two grandmothers, Queen Mary and the Countess of Strathmore (the Duchess's mother) while they set out in January 1927 on their six months tour of Australia and New Zealand. That first lesson in the duties of State passed unnoticed at the time over the fair-curled head of the baby Princess, who was happy enough spending the spring and summer days at Buckingham Palace, and at St. Paul's Walden, her other grandparents' home in Hertfordshire: it was the Duke and Duchess who felt the parting, able to watch their daughter's first developments only through the medium of photographs and lengthy nursery reports sent them by the two grandmothers and by the head nurse Mrs. Knight. But not long afterwards, the Duchess would tell her baby about the journey "Mummy and Daddy" had made and describe the wonderful things they had seen, gradually explaining to her why it was that she had had to be left behind. While her parents were away, the little Princess learned to utter her first word: it was "Mummy", and when the Duke and Duchess reached Buckingham Palace after the ceremonial drive through London that marked the end of their long tour of Empire, Queen Mary had her granddaughter there to meet them, to use her carefully learned word for the first time to her real "Mummy" instead of to her photograph.

Queen Victoria let it be known in after life that, though there had been many happy moments in her youthful period of training and education at Kensington Palace, it was not a period to which she could ever look back with feelings of unalloyed pleasure. One of her very earliest recollections, it is recorded, was of playing with the gold badge of the Garter belonging to Bishop Fisher of Salisbury, then Prelate of the Most Noble Order, and not much later she had to face what to our minds would be the intolerable ordeal of taking breakfast in the open with her mother, in full view of the strollers in Kensington Gardens.

At the last of her father's Camps: at Abergeldie near Balmoral, the month before the war began.

Modern views on the natural rights of Royalty to have some of their privacy respected spared Princess Elizabeth that rather peculiar early introduction to the duty of appearing at ease in front of a crowd, and the days of her early training passed pleasantly and happily. But the railings round the gardens behind Hamilton Place, within the Park at Hyde Park Corner, became a regular afternoon rendezvous for Londoners who wanted to see Royalty at play in the years from 1928 onwards, for it was into these gardens, behind her home at 145, Piccadilly, that the Princess was taken daily, when the weather allowed, for exercise and play. Provincial relatives visiting London would be taken to the Gardens to stand for an hour or more for a glimpse of a white-shawled baby. Business men from the Dominions were charged by their wives to make it their duty to see the Princess on one of her outings, and would write home long and glowing (though perhaps not always entirely truthful) accounts of what they had seen through the railings. A little later, King George gave orders for one of the pair-horse landaus from the Royal Mews to be sent across to Piccadilly in the afternoon, to take the Princess for a drive round the Serpentine, a change in the Royal routine that drew bigger crowds than ever to see the baby. The Princess was a quick, observant child, and it did not take her long to grasp that the people she saw in the Park were anxious to see her. Obligingly, she would sit up on her nurse's knee, smiling and waving her little hand, to the delight of the crowds, and to the amusement of the straight-faced liveried Royal footmen sitting behind her.

Such precocious Royal gestures were definitely not encouraged, for it was the explicit wish of the Duke and Duchess that their daughter should be brought up unspoiled by too early recognition of the position she undoubtedly enjoyed as the Empire's Baby. But it was obviously useless to attempt to disguise from her that the crowds *did* gather

c

round to see her when she went out, while her friend and playmate from next-door, the daughter of Lord and Lady Allendale, could go out as often as she pleased, without attracting any crowds. Thus it was while she was still quite a baby that she learned she was a Princess; that though her father's house, with its tall, black, double doors and the brown-carpeted hall, where the two great ivory tusks of the elephant he had shot in Uganda stood on either side of the steps, was a private house, her grandfather's house, whose grey walls she could see from her nursery windows, was a Palace; and that her grandfather, whose bearded face was always smiling when he saw her, was a King and an Emperor. But if, as the Duchess read her fairy stories with their tales of Princesses who invariably "lived happily ever after", she remarked that she was a Princess herself, her mother would gently remind her that she was a real life Princess, not one in a fairy-tale, and real-life Princesses, though they might make their lives happy, had lots of duties and tasks to perform which did not fall to their Royal sisters of fairyland.

In little ways like that, Princess Elizabeth was gradually accustomed to her future. Sometimes, as on her fourth birthday, which she spent at Windsor, she would be permitted to make a minor appearance in public. On that day, she solemnly "took the salute" from the Scots Guards, as they marched away after the changing of the Guard, with her elder boy cousins, the two sons of the Princess Royal (Viscount Lascelles and the Hon. Gerald Lascelles), whom she already knew were not Princes, though they, too, strangely enough, were the King's grandsons, standing a little behind her. The holiday crowds—it was Eastertide—cheered her, and running to the gates, she smiled at them, and waved de-lightedly.

Adventures of that kind were carefully watched and balanced so that there should be no over-emphasis on that side of life for the little girl. One day at the Royal Tourna-ment, that fascinating display of Service prowess which used to delight pre-war London, Princess Elizabeth was sitting in the Royal Box with Queen Mary. The crowds were waiting to see the Royal party leave, and the Princess was very conscious of the fact. She ventured to remark on it to her grandmother, telling the Queen how pleased all the people "will be to see me". That was enough for Queen Mary, who readily recognised the symptoms of self-importance, even in her beloved granddaughter. "Take the Princess out through the back, put her in a taxi, and take her to her home," she ordered one of the footmen, and away Princess Elizabeth went, to learn yet another rule of Royal behaviour.

Besides her mother and her grandmother, there was another woman, in a humbler sphere, who had a great influence on the development of Princess Elizabeth's character, to whom must justly be given some of the credit, too, for bringing both the Royal sisters up with an understanding of the value of manners, those outward symbols of an inward grace which William of Wykeham declared "makyeth man" and which assuredly may make, or mar, Princes and Princesses.

She was "Alla".

"Alla" was the name by which the Queen and both her daughters knew the late Mrs. Clara Cooper Knight, who, after growing old in the Queen's own service, spent some of the happiest years of her life as chief nurse to the Princesses. "Mrs." Knight—she had the title by the old-fashioned courtesy of "below-stairs", for she was never married—was the daughter of a yeoman farmer on the estates of the Queen's father, the Earl of Strathmore, at St. Paul's Walden, in Hertfordshire. As a girl of seventeen, she became under-nursery

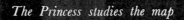
The Princess studies the map

maid, helping to look after the then Lady Elizabeth Bowes-Lyon. It was Lady Elizabeth's baby attempts to pronounce her nursery maid's name of Clara which resulted in "Alla", the designation which clung to her throughout the years. Between mistress and maid, a sincere and devoted attachment sprang up, an attachment which was to last right up to "Alla's" sudden death at Sandringham just after Christmas, 1945. The Queen and "Alla" understood each other perfectly, and the Queen knew that the upbringing of her daughters in all domestic matters could be in no better hands, nor could there be anyone else who would so exactly and intuitively carry out her own ideas and wishes, when State duties took her away from her children. One of the many things which Mrs. Knight knew very well was that the Queen wished her daughters to be brought up strictly and properly, with no laxity just because their father was King of England, but rather the reverse. So it was that "Alla", adoring slave of her young charges as she might be, always saw to it that they brushed and folded their clothes before going to bed as little girls, that they changed their shoes after a winter's day walk, in a word, that they took care of things and were not wasteful or neglectful.

That early training and the ingrained habits of tidiness it induced have never been forgotten by the Princesses, even though to-day their clothes are looked after by a maid.

When Mrs. Knight died, the Queen and the two Princesses made the long journey from Sandringham in Norfolk to St. Paul's Walden in Hertfordshire to attend her funeral, a very marked expression of the regard in which they held this faithful woman who had given them a lifetime's devotion.

The Queen wrote on the card tied to her wreath of violets, "In loving and thankful memory from Elizabeth R." The Princesses, on their wreath of mixed flowers, tied a card inscribed, "In loving memory of Alla, from Elizabeth and Margaret."

As the time for more serious lessons approached, the future education of the Royal heiress of the third generation became a topic of paramount importance to be discussed at Royal family councils, and even to be considered by the Cabinet. It was, as has already been indicated, the firm conviction of the Duke and Duchess of York that their daughter should be brought up in as normal a manner as possible, but that she should not go to any of the fashionable girls' schools. There were several reasons operating to bring them to this decision. For one thing the choice of one school rather than another might have been regarded as invidious, and might well have provoked minor jealousies. For another, the selection of schoolmates for a girl who, even then, could easily be envisaged as the future Queen, might have made difficulties. Weightier still was the drawback that no ordinary girls' school curriculum would include all the subjects that it was felt one in the direct line of succession should study: nor would it be possible to give the desired and necessary emphasis to certain subjects of particular importance to the Princess without seriously disrupting the scheme of study for other girls at the school.

So, with the complete agreement of King George (necessary, since the reigning sovereign has a constitutional right to prescribe the education of members of the Royal family) and Queen Mary, and, with the approval of the Government of the day, who, traditionally, have a right to be informed of the educational progress of those in close proximity to the throne, it was decided that Princess Elizabeth should, for the time being, at any rate, be educated privately at home. This arrangement, which became a permanency, gave the added advantage of keeping the Princess within the family circle where, by example

She knows the good points of a farm horse : with the King at Sandringham at harvest time.

and precept, she could continue to absorb, as she had been doing up till then, the ways and manners of the Royal family. All that remained was to find a suitable person to be her instructress. Naturally, it was the Princess's mother who began to search for such a person, and her eyes at once turned to a young Scots woman in the household of her sister, Lady Rose, who was married to Admiral Earl Granville (now Governor of Northern Ireland). This was Miss Marion Crawford, a twenty-five year old native of Dunfermline, who, after leaving Dunfermline High School, had gone on to take an honours degree at Edinburgh University. She had been governess first in the family of Lord Elgin, then had come to be governess to Lady Mary Leveson-Gower, the Duchess's niece. Lady Granville recommended her daughter's governess very highly, and in 1933, when the Princess was seven years old, Miss Crawford came to the Duchess to start her daughter on the highroad of learning. She is still with the Princess to-day.

"Crawfie" as she quickly came to be known in the Royal family circle, was an ideal choice. Quiet, reserved in manner, with a wide and far-ranging intelligence, she combined the qualities of firmness—very necessary in the case of a highly self-confident Princess—with an affectionate charm that won her Royal pupil's heart from the beginning. Now that the Princess is a grown young woman, "Crawfie" remains one of her closest intimates, one of her most trusted confidantes and advisers; but no one outside the Royal circle ever hears "Crawfie" talk about her Royal charge. She has always been, and still is, content to remain in the background, shrinking from any form of publicity, and yet forming a most valuable link between the Princess and the outer world.

Keen on foreign travel, she would spend her holidays abroad, where no one meeting the self-contained, brown-haired Scotswoman who seemed to know so much of local history, would dream that she had charge of the education of the future Queen of

England. When she came home, the Princess would hear from her of life in other countries, gaining a vicarious, but valuable, insight into the ways of other lands. Baroness Lehzen, who filled a like office to Queen Victoria, used to address her Royal pupil as "Madam", and treated her, to judge from contemporary accounts, in a manner that, to modern taste, seems a little priggish. No such charge could be brought against Miss Crawford. Between her and her two pupils—for Princess Margaret, a few years later, came to join her sister's studies—there has always existed a most happy and natural relationship unstrained in any way. To-day, on public occasions, she will address the Princess with the "Ma'am" of formality, but in the class room, it was simply "Princess", or in earlier days, more simply still "Elizabeth". Princess Elizabeth, and the empire at large, owe

The Princess explores London's river : aboard the P.L.A. launch with Queen Mary she takes a trip down the Thames.

a great debt to this Scotswoman of sterling character and uprightness, who has taught her much besides mere book reading, and no assessment of the Princess could be complete without tribute to the good influence of Miss Crawford.

History, geography, arithmetic, algebra, English grammar and literature were among the Princess's early studies, and of these, history was easily a first favourite, enlivened often by stories not to be found in the history books, stories of family connections and ancestors who had played their part and left their mark on the European scene. Shakespeare, too, was made more vivid for the Princess when she came to read Macbeth, and could so easily conjure up the worn steps of the circular stone staircase, the deep embrasured windows of Glamis Castle, her summer holiday home, as a background for the sonorous periods of the great drama: or realise, when she read Henry V, that it was of her own ancestor-King that

Shakespeare wrote. All these aids to Royal learning, which fitted so easily and well into the scheme of education at home, would have been a hundred times more difficult at school.

But though her lessons were done in the friendly atmosphere of her own home, in the familiar surroundings of an upstairs room at Piccadilly, set aside for exclusive use as a schoolroom, the Princess was not allowed any more laxity—indeed rather less—than girls at school. School hours were regularly set, and regularly adhered to, and, by an early and a wise decision of the Duke and Duchess of York, were regarded as having first and overriding call on the Royal pupil's time. It is easy to imagine what confusion the Princess's schoolwork could easily have fallen into had this rule not been applied, and had, instead, public outings and functions been allowed to interfere with the programme of lessons. That was emphatically not the way the Duke and Duchess wanted their daughter to be trained, and Miss Crawford saw to it that pressure from any and every quarter to break into the educational routine was stoutly and strongly resisted.

With a naturally quick brain and a lively intelligence, the Princess profited to the full under this system of disciplined, though not forced, education. She showed an early aptitude for English, a liking for, and skill in, composition, that remain with her to-day so that, if, at any time in the future, any of her writings are made public—not that there is much likelihood of this happening—her prose style would show her a worthy descendant of Queen Victoria, to whose clarity of thought and vigour of expression (if slightly marred by a predilection for italics and underlinings) her published letters are sufficient testimony. She was, in the main, a diligent pupil, slightly impatient to advance at a faster pace than was always considered wise, but with a memory so retentive, and a mental grasp so eager, of any subject in which she was really interested, that the greater speed was many times justified.

To the Duchess, who had been taught French in her early infancy—a happy circumstance that enables the Queen of England to-day to talk with ease, fluency and an almost faultless accent to the citizens of France in their own language—it seemed that the earlier her daughter began to learn a second language, the better. Princess Elizabeth began to lisp French words nearly as soon as she started to speak English, learning them at her mother's knee, an early foundation which caused her first native French instructress to wonder at the purity of her accent. "French only" periods, including meal-times, were the frequent rule in the Royal nursery. During these, anything said in any other language was ignored, a practice which continued until quite recent days. The Princess still has, as one of her close friends and personal companions, a French lady, Madame la Comtesse de Bellaigue, who became attached to the Royal household as senior French tutor and companion to the Princess during the war.

To-day, French is a natural second language to the Princess. She can read, write and express herself as clearly in French as in her native English, and has a wider and deeper acquaintance with French literature and verse than many Frenchmen. She is familiar with the works of the great classic masters, Molière, Racine, Corneille, to name but a few, and with the writings of modern French authors as well. She can quote long passages from Du Bellay, Malherbe, Lamartine and Hugo, as well as many of the sonnets and rodels of Villon and Ronsard. When she broadcast to the children of newly-liberated Belgium early in 1945, so perfect was her delivery, so pure and free from English accent

She sees her tutor knighted: Dr. Henry Marten, Provost of Eton, kneels to the King on the College Chapel steps

her enunciation, that a famous actor of the Comédie Française, who had coached novice speakers on the BBC's European transmissions during the war, said to me as he listened, "Elle fait à marveille: on croit vraiement c'est une Française qui parle." Tears rolled down that famous French actor's cheeks as he listened to the simple words of the eighteen year old British Princess expressing her country's thanks to the children of Belgium for their Christmas gift of toys to the boys and girls of Britain. When the day comes for the Princess to visit Belgium and other French-speaking countries of Europe, she will be surprised at the number of men and women who yield their hearts to her at the memory of that one short radio talk.

That French should come easily to the Princess is not surprising. Not only her mother, but also her aunt, the Princess Royal, spoke the language so well as a girl that at the early age of twelve she drew from the French Ambassador of the day congratulations on her "charming and fluent" pronunciation of his language.

French was not the only language Princess Elizabeth learned in her schoolroom. When war began, she was already well advanced with her German studies, and a hard decision had to be reached. Should these studies be discontinued, on the narrow precedent of the 1914–18 war, because we were again at war, this time with Nazi Germany, or should the Princess continue normally in the course set for her? In spite of the risk of ill-founded criticism, which, happily, was not forthcoming, the King decided that the language of Schiller and Goethe was much greater and more lasting than the ephemeral Third Reich of Herr Hitler, and he could see no need to deprive his daughter of a knowledge of the great storehouse of German literature merely because the present day users of that language were attempting to destroy the rest of civilisation. So the Princess continued to study German, though not, perhaps, with quite the same enthusiasm as she displayed for French!

The Princess was never allowed to imagine that there is any easy Royal road to learning even for those of Royal birth. She had to devote as much care and time to her three favourite subjects, English, history and French, as to others, like arithmetic and algebra, which she absorbed more slowly and with less zest. In the days when she sat alone in her classroom at Piccadilly, or later, when she sat with Princess Margaret in the schoolroom at Buckingham Palace where her father and uncles had done their early studies, the Royal pupil, just like any other girl, had to plough through the rules of grammar, to conjugate verbs, regular and irregular, to parse and analyse sentences, to memorise place names and battle dates. In her case, thoroughness of grounding was even more rigidly insisted on— and much more easy to enforce—than with a group of girls studying together. That does not mean that all lessons were made dull. On the contrary, Miss Crawford kept it as a guiding principle to make them all as interesting and stimulating as possible, and all sorts of outside aids were brought in to this end. Geography, for instance, which was not among the Princess's early favourites, was made more attractive by tales of the overseas visits of members of her family, and of course, the family motif ran through many of the early English history lessons. At Buckingham Palace there were many souvenirs of overseas visits and gifts from foreign visitors which served as starting points for interest in one country or another. This was particularly so, naturally, in the case of the Dominions and India, and the British colonies.

A rug which the Princess used for many years whenever she went out for a motor ride illustrates this aspect of the carefully planned training devised for her. The rug,

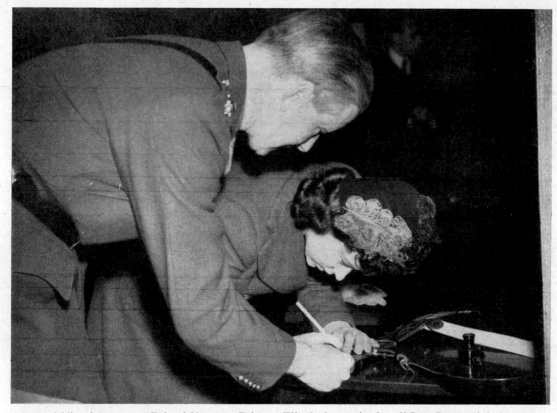

Adding honour to a Belt of Honour: Princess Elizabeth autographs a "Sam Browne" before presenting it to the best cadet at a Sandhurst passing-out parade.

of warm shaggy sheepskin, backed by thick blue cloth, looked ordinary enough, comfortably tucked round the Princess and whoever might be her companion in the car. The secret was on the back. Outlined in bold yellow stitching against the blue ground was an exact and accurate map of Australia, showing the divisions of the States and Territories, each with its name or initials. No one, using that mapped rug for any length of time, could help but have the contours of the Commonwealth engraved, almost unconsciously, on their mind.

Based on much the same educational principles, visits to the Tower of London, the museums of South Kensington, and other places of historical importance form a usual part of present day school-training. Princess Elizabeth and Princess Margaret had the advantage, when they made their round of such visits in the spring and early summer of 1939, while the King and Queen were away on their tour of Canada and their visit to the United States, of having their grandmother, Queen Mary, as their mentor and guide. Probably no one outside the regular staffs of the various museums has anything like such a deep and detailed knowledge of the historical exhibits, particularly those with Royal associations, in our great national collections, as has Queen Mary. She gladly consented to take her grandchildren on a "grand tour" of the London treasure houses, and enthusiastic accounts of all they had seen with her went from the Princesses across the Atlantic to the King and Queen. After hearing her tell them legends and stories of the past made vivid for them by what they saw, the Monument, Traitors' Gate at the Tower, the Elgin Marbles at the British Museum, and so on, the Royal sisters would go back to the drier side of their historical studies with renewed and invigorated zeal.

In the midst of all this serious preparation for the earnest life to come, the Princess remained a happy, unspoilt little girl, so natural and free from self-importance that even the great excitement of the coronation did not turn her head.

A couple of months after those never-to-be-forgotten festivities, Princess Elizabeth found herself one evening with Princess Margaret in their sleeping saloon on the Royal train, drawn up at the Euston platform awaiting the arrival of the King and Queen on their way north to Balmoral. The Princesses had been brought to the station early to be put to bed on the train at their usual time. A railway policeman, pacing the platform, after the Royal nurses had made their way to their own part of the train, was surprised to hear a tapping, regular and distinct, coming from the windows of the Royal train. Doubtless with some thoughts of madmen and train wreckers in mind, he approached the window more closely, to see the blind drawn back, and Princess Elizabeth trying to attract his attention. "Please, policeman, go and get us a comic paper to read," pleaded the heiress of England, holding out a shilling in her hand through the opened window. "Please!" There was nothing in his instructions telling him what to do in a case like this, so the slightly bewildered constable, not used to receiving direct Royal requests, walked off to the bookstall, purchased the "comics", and handed them through the window with the change to the very grateful eleven year-old inside.

But he did not pay for the papers with the Princess's shilling. He used another coin of his own for that, keeping the Royal shilling as a treasured souvenir.

Formal examinations, the Junior Oxford Locals, which her mother had passed as a young girl, and later, the Senior Schools, and Matriculation, were not, it was laid down, to come the Princess's way, since her studies were based on a more specialised plan, but the indispensable check that graded examinations at regular intervals give on school progress was obtained simply by the setting of papers designed especially for the Princess, yet based on the general average standard of her age. Consistently, she gained excellent marks, assessing her as definitely of above average intelligence, and these results were made the more reliable by the fact that steps were taken to see that the examiners did not always know whose papers they were marking.

The overall master plan for the Princess's education laid down in her earliest years by her father and mother, in agreement with King George V and Queen Mary, needed very little alteration, but soon the time came when more specialised and advanced studies called for extra tuition in addition to that of Miss Crawford. The claims of many eminent and leading figures in the scholastic world were given most careful review before this important choice was made. Finally, the King gave approval to the appointment as chief tutor to the Princess of one of the most highly regarded of living historians, Mr. (now Sir) Clarence Henry Kennett Marten, at that time Vice-Provost, now Provost, of Eton College, renowned alike for his profound knowledge of history both classical and modern, and for his individual and highly successful approach to the teaching of it.

That decision has never been regretted either by the King and Queen, by Sir Henry

The Princess shows she knows how to hold a baby at a visit to the Heritage Craft Schools for crippled children

Shelter from the Admiral's umbrella : Admiral Sir Geoffrey Layton, C.-in-C. Portsmouth, shows the Princess over Nelson's "Victory".

46

Marten, or by Princess Elizabeth. Seldom can a happier choice have been made. History, world history, British, European, American, political and economic history, is necessarily the subject of primary importance in the education of those to whose lot it must fall to take some part, greater or smaller, in the making of the history of the future. A sound basis of knowledge of the mistakes, as well as the successes of the past, is an essential to good judgement on the problems of the present, and it was the high task of the new tutor to see that the Princess was guided along the ways of learning in such fashion as to give her this qualification for wise decision on the multifarious problems that one day will be brought to her. The outward mark and sign of the success with which he has acquitted himself of that charge is to be found in the signal honour which the King did him when, on Sunday, March 4, 1945, he knighted him and invested him with the insignia of a Knight Commander of the Royal Victorian Order—the personal order of the Royal Family, bestowed only for direct and personal service to members of it, without recommendation from political quarters—on the steps of Eton College Chapel, in the open air, in full view of the Eton boys.

The deeper and more significant sign of his success lies in the finely trained brain with its deep background of accurate, well-digested knowledge, that is Princess Elizabeth's to-day.

Sir Henry, known to all Etonians as "Shee-Kay" from his own pronunciation of his initials, has been sixty years at Eton. He was educated at Eton and then at Balliol College, Oxford, where he took a First Class in Modern History. He returned to Eton in 1896 at the age of twenty-four, as an assistant master of brilliant young promise. He became successively a house master, Lower Master, from 1925–29, Vice Provost in 1929, and finally Provost in 1945. President of the Historical Association from 1929–31, he has written much about history and its teaching, and has played a major part in bringing about the modern attitude to history as a study of the vast, complex changes in, and the evolution of, human society, rather than an absorption in national movements and the duration of dynasties and the lives of Kings.

Some slight idea of the depth and variety of the Princess's studies may be gauged from the fact that such unusual, but vastly important, subjects as the history of British agriculture, and the theory and law of land tenure, were included among the special subjects which she studied under Sir Henry.

When Prince Albert Edward, afterwards King Edward VII, was eighteen, in 1859, his father, the Prince Consort, called a conference of educational leaders at Edinburgh, in May, to review the question of the future education of the heir to the throne. As a result, it was decided that the Prince should spend a time at both Oxford and Cambridge—thus avoiding any hurt to the feelings of either University—with a programme of study which the late Sir George Arthur described as a "colossal curriculum, with the addition of indigestible learning." Prince Albert Edward in after life, became famous for "knowing everything that is not in books, and little that is," perhaps as a revolt from this early attempt to cram too much bookish lore into his young mind.

That danger does not confront Princess Elizabeth. Though, as has been indicated, her studies and curriculum were at various stages the subject of family talks within the Royal circle, and though the Cabinet took a constant, if not a very close or detailed, interest in her educational progress, the mistake of putting the question of her future

With Princess Margaret in the West End

Three Royal ladies: Her Majesty the Queen with Princess Elizabeth and Princess Margaret, in printed summer frocks

Photograph by The Hon. M. W. Elphinstone

training to semi-public debate at a formal educational conference was never made, nor was there any attempt at forcing too much learning on her too quickly.

Yet the Princess who was eighteen in 1944, had problems to study which were certainly not the concern of her great-grandfather ninety-five years beforehand. American history, for example, was a closed book to Albert Edward when he went to the United States in 1859-60, and the history of the Dominion of Canada had yet to be written when he journeyed through it on that same tour *incognito* as "Lord Renfrew", for the British North America Act, under which the Dominion came into being, was still seven years distant in the future.

Princess Elizabeth has studied the history of each of the four great Dominions, as well as Indian history: and the economic and political development of each, as well. She has read—as too few of her father's subjects have read—Muzzey's "History of the United States", and many other books and papers on the history of the Republic besides that great standard work. She is probably better acquainted with the history and development of the United States than a good many American girls of her age, and she is certainly the very first heir to the British throne to be brought up with a full understanding and realisation of the growth and rise to power of our great sister democracy. Even as late as the King's own young days, the teaching of American history was apt to stop short at a sketchy, and not always accurate, account of the War of Independence of 1775-82, and the Civil War of 1860-65. Princess Elizabeth's teaching and reading went far beyond the Boston Tea Party and the march of Stonewall Jackson, deep into the causes underlying the two struggles, the effects of the outcome of each, and the general progress of the American people after them. Nor was she taught to read history through rose-coloured glasses. The Boer war, its causes and effects, the French problem in Canada, and other Dominion difficulties past and present have been put before her without disguise.

Economics, economic history, and British constitutional history, are all subjects in which the Princess is well versed. Her reading has been wide and catholic, ranging in English from Shakespeare's plays, Chaucer's *Canterbury Tales*, the poems of Keats, Coleridge, Browning and Tennyson, to Dickens, Scott, Trollope, Stevenson, Conan Doyle and John Buchan, in French from Daudet's *Lettres de Mon Moulin* to Foncin's *Geographie Historique*.

Nowadays, regular school hours are no longer desired, or even possible, for the Princess has too many other calls on her time. But she still continues a certain amount of reading of a post-graduate nature in some of the subjects, history prime among them, which have always been her special interests.

The fact that she was never subject to any "cramming" can best be seen from her school timetable as a girl. Lessons began at 9.30 precisely, after schoolroom breakfast which she took alone with her governess. At eleven o'clock, there was a "break" for walking or riding—mostly in Windsor Great Park—with lessons resumed again at 11.45.

In the afternoon, the programme varied with the season and the weather. At least two hours of work were expected of the Royal pupil, but often these would be devoted to subjects of a lighter nature, drawing, or, in summer, sketching out of doors. That was the regime under Miss Crawford and her women teachers for French and German. Later, when her studies under Sir Henry Marten became more serious and intensified, the hours were prolonged, the afternoons devoted more to serious reading—though much of this was done in the open air—and a good deal of the evenings spent in written preparation.

Never interfering with those to whom she had entrusted her daughter's education, but always watchful in the background, the Queen supervised every detail of the education of Princess Elizabeth, and still acts in the same way to Princess Margaret whose training is following much the same course as that of her sister.

One other, and most important, aspect of the training of the Princess concerns religion. Quite apart from the fact that when she comes to Queenship, the Princess will occupy a special position, carry special responsibilities, as head of the Established Church, she has been brought up by her parents in the simple, Christian faith that is theirs. Scriptural history and studies, under the guidance of Canon Crawley, of St. George's Chapel, Windsor, took a prominent place in her early studies. In matters of religion, it is the home and family influence that are most important, and in no home in the Empire is there a couple of more sincere and devout religious persuasion than the King and Queen. Regular attendance at church is, and has always been, a dominant feature in the life of the Royal family circle, and it is a rare thing indeed for Princess Elizabeth to miss morning service, no matter where she may be.

She was christened on May 29, 1926, in the private chapel of Buckingham Palace, the chapel which, fifteen years later, was to be shattered by a German bomb.

Traditional observance and high ceremony properly surrounded this occasion of great import. The fair-haired baby girl who one day might occupy her grandfather's position as the temporal head of the Church of England, was baptised by the Archbishop of York (the late Lord Lang of Lambeth), assisted by Prebendary Percival, Precentor of the Chapels Royal and Domestic Chaplain to the King.

Her four grandparents, the King and Queen and the Earl and Countess of Strathmore, her parents, the Duke and Duchess of York, her uncles and aunt, the Prince of Wales, Prince Henry and Princess Mary, and a number of other close relatives, were the only witnesses of the ceremony, at which the choir of the Chapel Royal sang. She had six sponsors, King George and Queen Mary, Princess Mary, the veteran Duke of Connaught, last surviving son of Queen Victoria, the Earl of Strathmore, and her maternal aunt, Lady Elphinstone.

Her christening robe of old ivory lace was itself an heirloom of Royalty, for it had been worn by four future sovereigns of England in turn at their christenings, Queen Victoria, King Edward VII, King George V, and King Edward VIII, as well as by the Empress Frederick, Queen Victoria's daughter. Water for the Royal baptism had been brought from the River Jordan, as was the custom at all Royal christenings, and the "Lily Font", a gold bowl used at the christenings of all Queen Victoria's descendants born in this country, was brought to the Palace from Windsor Castle for the occasion.

Sixteen years later, after receiving a special course of instruction from her early religious mentor, Canon Crawley, the Princess was confirmed, in the tiny circular private chapel at Windsor Castle. Dr. Lang, now Archbishop of Canterbury, assisted by the Dean of Windsor, Dr. Baillie, administered the rite, on March 28, 1942. Afterwards, the Archbishop preached a short sermon, in which he reminded the young Princess of the high and dread responsibilities of the station to which it had pleased God to call her. Princess Elizabeth took her first communion privately on the following Sunday.

CHAPTER THREE

Her Place in the Constitution

ON the evening of Thursday, August 21, 1930, a heavy thunderstorm broke over the little town of Forfar, in the county of Angus, Scotland. Lightning flashed across the greying summer sky, rolls of thunder reverberated across the vale of Strathmore, echoed back from the forest-clad hills. Within the massive stone walls of Glamis Castle, the ancient home of Macbeth, whose name Shakespeare wove for ever into the pattern of British history, the thunder seemed to those waiting to provide a sombre accompaniment to the great event that was at last taking place after many long days of dragging expectancy.

Through the pelting rain, a fast-driven car came to the tall iron gates, blazoned with the arms of the Earls of Strathmore, its headlights throwing into sudden prominence the strange "Beasts of Glamis" whose stone-carved effigies figure the outer walls of the Castle grounds. Police, their flat caps, with blue and white diced bands of Scotland, and their oilskin capes dripping with water, saluted as the car passed. In it was the stocky figure of Mr. J. R. Clynes, the former cotton worker who was then His Majesty's Principal Secretary of State for Home Affairs. He had just been summoned by telephone to Glamis Castle from "the Bonnie Hoose o' Airlie"—otherwise Airlie Castle, half a dozen miles away, near Kirriemuir—where he was staying with the Dowager Countess of Airlie. The little crowd of villagers and Pressmen waiting outside the Castle gates knew, when they saw him drive in, that the hour they had been so long awaiting had arrived, for the mission that had brought Mr. Clynes some five hundred miles from Whitehall to one remote Scottish Castle, where for three weeks he had been transacting the business of the Home Office under some difficulties, and now sent him hurrying through the storm to another, was to carry out his constitutional duty of testifying to the birth of a new grandchild to King George V, who, boy or girl, would be in direct line of succession to the Throne.

Until fairly recent times, this duty which dates back to the days when Royal changelings might be foisted on the people, had been carried out to the letter by successive Home Secretaries, who were compelled to be present at the actual birth, or at least, in an adjoining room. But this distasteful task had been lightened at the suggestion of the Prince Consort, when the future Edward VII was born at Buckingham Palace in 1841, and the immediate personal presence of the Home Secretary has not been deemed necessary since then, though he must be within close call, and his department remains, to this day, the official channel through which all Royal births are announced.

Mr. Clynes was not surprised therefore when the Duke of York met him at the great door of Glamis with the news that the baby was already born. But he was eager, as the whole nation and empire were eager, to know if it was a Prince or a Princess that he was about to see. The Duke told him it was a daughter.

That one word meant all the difference to the future of Princess Elizabeth. Had the Duchess's second child been a son, Princess Elizabeth of York would have been no

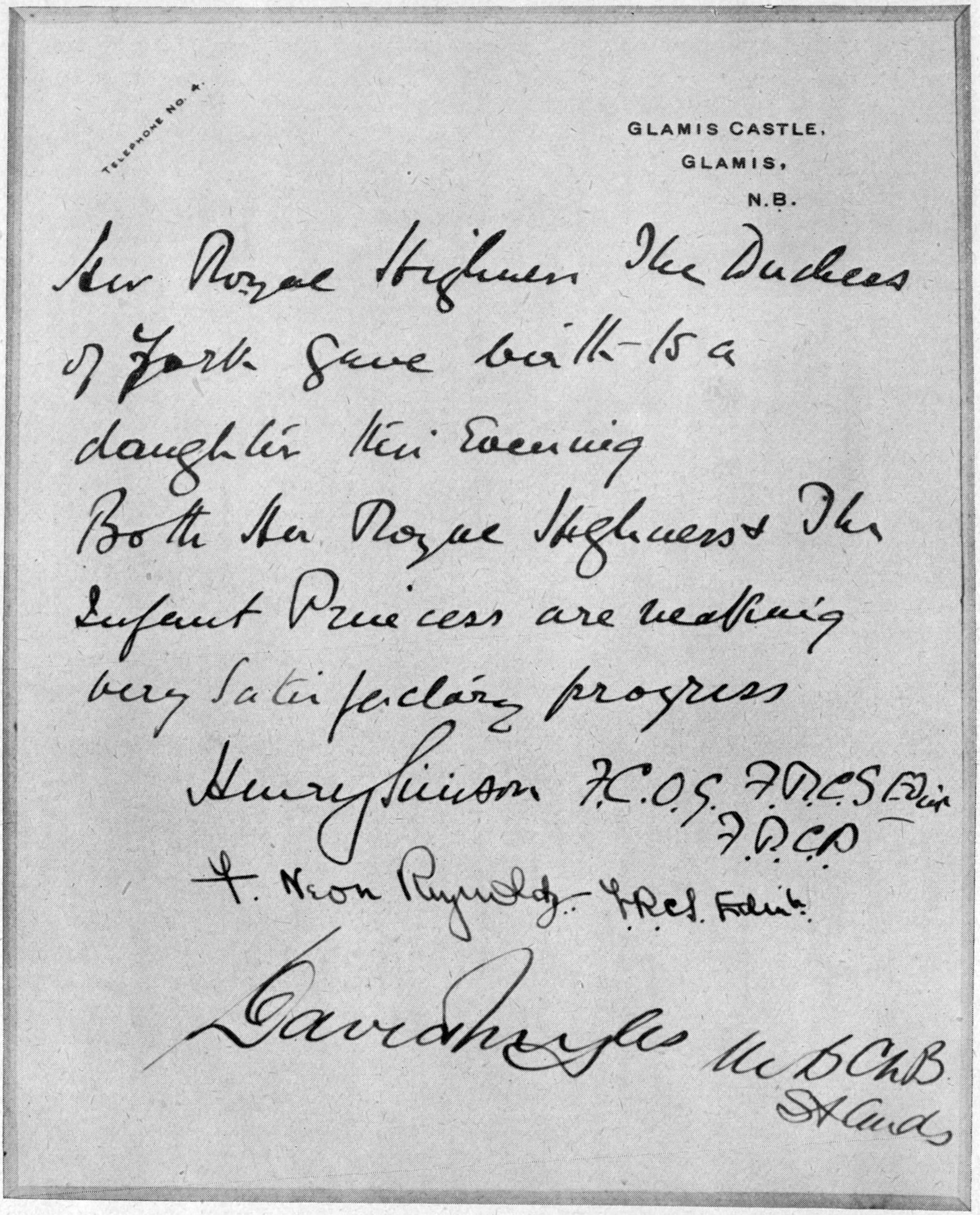

GLAMIS CASTLE,
GLAMIS,
N.B.

Her Royal Highness The Duchess
of York gave birth to a
daughter this evening

Both Her Royal Highness & The
Infant Princess are making
very satisfactory progress

Henry Simson F.C.O.G. F.R.C.S. Edin
F.O.C.P.

+ Neon Reynolds F.R.C.S. Edin.

David Myles M.B.Ch.B.
St Andrs

The bulletin that made history : photographed from the original written at Glamis on the night of Princess Margaret's birth, August 21, 1930.

longer third, but fourth, in succession to the crown her grandfather still wore, and this would have changed, drastically changed, her life from then on. With a sister, and not a brother, added to her family, she remained the first of the new generation in the line of succession, and, in a sense, her training for the responsibilities of future Queenship began to take more definite shape from that moment.

The three doctors attending the Duchess, Dr. David Myles, a St. Andrews man, who was the local physician, the late Sir Henry Simson, the gynaecologist, and Mr. F. Neon Reynolds, the surgeon and anaesthetist, sat down to write their bulletin, while the Duke sent off telegrams to the King and Queen, aboard the Royal yacht at Cowes, and to other members of the Royal family, and Mr. Clynes completed his constitutional duty by despatching a telegram conveying the news to the Lord Mayor of London.

Meanwhile, the growing crowd at the Castle gates were becoming impatient. They still knew nothing, and it was a full hour later before the doctors' bulletin was read out in the little village street of Glamis, to be flashed by telephone to the waiting newspaper offices in London, standing by with their presses held. For the long period of waiting, the importance attaching to the sex of the new baby, the romantic setting for the birth, had all combined to bring public interest to excitement point.

There was a certain feeling of regret at the absence of a new male in the direct line of succession: but there was general satisfaction that the four-years-old Princess, who had already won herself a place as the nation's darling, was not to be displaced by a baby Prince.

After the high-spirited celebrations in Glamis village and the neighbourhood had died down, after the bonfires lit to mark the birth of the first Royal Princess to be born in Scotland for 300 years had burned out, students of genealogy began to busy themselves with the question of whether the arrival of the new Princess of York did not, in fact, alter the position of her elder sister in relation to the succession. Basing their arguments on the legal position that the law of primogeniture applies in this country only to male heirs of private estates, they put forward the theory that the two Royal sisters shared equal rights, just as is the case with two daughters of a peer or other landowner, however great the difference in their ages. In such a case, the title, according to the ancient law of succession, goes into abeyance, and the property is shared equally.

To-day, when Princess Elizabeth is universally recognised as the sole heiress to the throne, with her sister, Princess Margaret, next after her in succession, the question may seem remote and academic, but at the time, and, indeed, throughout the next ten years, it was raised repeatedly in various quarters, without any really authoritative pronouncement being made. Genealogists, laboriously searching the records, found that the problem of which of two Royal sisters should succeed had arisen in the past, to be settled by specific Acts of Parliament, as in the case of Princess Mary and Princess Elizabeth, the daughters of Henry VIII, and in the case of the two daughters of James II, Mary and Anne, whose succession to the crown in that order was determined under the Bill of Rights. Hence, they concluded, the succession to the Throne had always followed the same rules as applied to real property until the reforms made under Lord Birkenhead as Lord Chancellor, which meant that the two Princesses would inherit equally as co-heiresses. Constitutional lawyers, realising that such a position would be intolerable, urged the necessity for passing legislation to settle the order of succession and to establish the constitutional position of the elder Princess. By one of those fascinating twists of legal precedent, the question of equal inheritance did not, it was stressed, arise in the case of the Crown of Scotland because the interpretation of the Scots peerage law allowed an elder daughter to succeed in preference to her younger sister. This, again, could be challenged on the legitimate score that the Act of Union, passed in 1706, included provision for the terms of the Act of Settlement of 1700 (which ruled that the Crown, and "all honours, styles, titles, regalities, prerogatives, powers, jurisdictions and authorities" should descend through Princess Sophia, Electress of Hanover and granddaughter of James I, to "the heirs of her body being Protestants") to apply equally to Scotland, thenceforth united with England in the Kingdom of Great Britain.

In the next editions of Debrett, and Burke's Peerage, (for 1931) the position of the new Princess of the House of Windsor, H.R.H. Margaret Rose of York, was mentioned. It was stated by Burke that "As a result of an inquiry into the constitutional position, the Royal Princess has been declared fourth in succession to the throne" while Debrett made the point in a similiar way. But this did not satisfy the constitutional purists. Law Officers of the Crown had studied the question very closely, on the orders of King George V, and had reported privately that the right of Princess Elizabeth to succeed before her younger sister was unimpeachable and needed no special Act of Parliament to confirm it. But their findings had neither been reported by the Prime Minister of the day, nor otherwise made public.

When the Duke of York succeeded as King George VI, the matter became of much greater urgency, as the Princess was now the immediate heiress to the throne. Two months after the accession, the question was finally cleared up through the medium of question-and-answer in the House of Commons.

On January 28, 1937, Mr. Geoffrey Mander, Liberal M.P. for Wolverhampton (East), asked the Home Secretary (Sir John, now Viscount, Simon) whether it was proposed to introduce legislation to amend the Act of Settlement with a view to making clear that the Princess Elizabeth was the sole heir to the Throne, and did not share it jointly with her sister on the analogy of the Peerage Law. Sir John's reply was a declaration of first rate constitutional importance, for it settled the question of succession without room for further quibbling. He said: "No, Sir: there is no reason to do so. His Majesty's Government are advised that there is no doubt that in the present circumstances Her Royal Highness the Princess Elizabeth would succeed to the Throne as sole heir."

From then on, no one has been able to question the undoubted position of the King's elder daughter as his heiress presumptive. Yet, in the minds of the general public, as distinct from those who make a study of the constitution, there still seems to remain room for doubt of another kind, doubt, in this case, as to the exact implication of the phrase "Heiress Presumptive". This doubt can be quickly and easily cleared up. Had a son been born to Their Majesties at any time since the accession, he would have been, at birth, Duke of Cornwall, and *Heir Apparent* to the Throne, thus displacing his elder sister as next in succession to her father, and making Princess Margaret third instead of second, in the line. That is a hypothetical, or presumptive case, and it is precisely on the presumption that there will be no male child of a Sovereign that his daughter remains his heir, unless and until a son is born. Princess Elizabeth can therefore never become Heiress Apparent, for as long as her father lives, the legal and constitutional presumption that he might have a son must be maintained.

It is for the same reason, namely that the law must always take into account the possibility of the birth of further children during the father's lifetime, that the title of the Dukedom of Cornwall, together with the rich estates that appertain to it, cannot be bestowed by the King on Princess Elizabeth. They must remain in abeyance for the use of any future first-born son of the Sovereign.

If no son is born to his present Majesty, the Royal Dukedom will remain vested in the Crown until such time as there is a son born to the reigning sovereign of the day.

This question of a new title became a matter of public interest as the Princess's eighteenth birthday approached. For Royalty, eighteen is an age of special import, for, as will be seen later, it is then that Royalty enters into majority of a limited kind, and in consequence, there was a great deal of speculation about what action the King might take to mark the occasion. In many different quarters, the suggestion was mooted that His Majesty should bestow a new title on his daughter, in recognition of her new status. In Wales, where the direct connection of the Principality with the Royal House dates back for more than six hundred years to the day when Edward I made his infant son the first Prince of Wales, there was tremendous enthusiasm for a proposal that the ancient custom of reserving that title for a male heir should be waived, so that Princess Elizabeth might henceforth be known as the Princess of Wales. Welsh men and women of all degrees gave the idea their support.

Welsh M.P.s, led by Sir Henry Morris-Jones, backed the suggestion, and the local council at Pwllheli, in Caernarvonshire, went a step further by passing a resolution on August 23, 1943, asking the Prime Minister to recommend to His Majesty that the title of Princess of Wales should be created and bestowed on his elder daughter. There was, protagonists of the idea claimed, some shadowy precedent for such an act in 1525, when Princess Mary was sent to Ludlow Castle to exercise the powers of Princess of Wales, though she was never formally invested with the title.

How much, if any, of his time Mr. Winston Churchill was able to spare from his planning and direction of the war to attend to this domestic, but none the less important matter, has not been revealed, but the Pwllheli Council received a reply regretting that their suggestion was not possible.

It was not possible for exactly the same reason which rendered it impossible for Princess Elizabeth to be made Duchess of Cornwall: the Princess of Wales is a title reserved exclusively for the wife of a Prince of Wales, who must be the eldest son of the reigning sovereign.

Eager to revive their close association with the Royal house by some other means when the first had failed, the loyal folk of the Principality put forward a new suggestion, this time that the King might create an entirely new Welsh title, and make his daughter Duchess of Cymru, thus incorporating into a Royal title the ancient Celtic name for Wales: or alternatively, Duchess of Gwalia, with the new title descending always to the eldest daughter of the Sovereign, as that of the Prince of Wales does to the eldest son.

Undoubtedly these, and all other suggestions of a sensible character—there were one or two which scarcely merited inclusion in this category—were the subject of careful attention by the King and His Majesty's advisers. One which certainly must have been numbered among these emanated from Scotland, where staunch loyalists wanted to tie yet another and a new bond between their ancient Kingdom and the Princess who one

The Princess wearing her Coronet:

day may rule over it as part of the realm of Great Britain. They bluntly suggested that if, as seemed to be the case, she could not be made Princess of Wales because of the prior claims of a possible and as yet unborn Prince, there was nothing of that kind to prevent her being made Princess of Scotland.

It was the passing of the Regency Act of 1943, which both clarified, and in part superseded, the former Regency Act of 1937, that gave impetus to public interest in the Princess's title, and prompted so many bodies and individuals to put forward their various suggestions. The 1943 Act mentioned the Princess by name, and affected her directly, for under it she was empowered with an important and high function of State, the qualification to act as one of the Councillors of State to whom the Royal powers are delegated in the absence of the Sovereign from the Kingdom, or his inability through illness or other cause to attend to the affairs of the nation. Suddenly, people, who had been accustomed to thinking of the Princess as a little girl, a sentiment which the strict

on the Palace balcony after the Coronation

seclusion and privacy of her early upbringing had done much to foster, began to realise that she was fast growing up, and would shortly begin to take her place in public life. This, if any, was surely the time for a change in her title to be made. But, having passed all the suggestions submitted to him in careful review, having given due consideration to each, having weighed the arguments for a change, having examined all the precedents governing the case, the King, in his wisdom, decided to make no alteration in his daughter's title. It was as Princess Elizabeth that she had grown up, it was as Princess Elizabeth that the Empire and the world at large knew her, and it seemed, perhaps, too late to make a change. The suggestion that she should be Princess of Wales had been ruled out of court, the title of Princess of Scotland might have conveyed some slight and unseemly preference for one section of the United Kingdom over the others, the title of Duchess of Cymru could scarcely have recommended itself to eighteen-year-old Elizabeth, who would have had to yield up her familiar Royal title of Princess for one borne by others not of Royal rank, and there were equal objections to the various alternatives that had been put forward, so that, after the period of eager interest had passed, reflection at leisure produced general agreement that His Majesty had in this, as in so many other matters, ranging from the bestowal of the George Cross on the Island of Malta to the gift of a sword to Stalingrad, once again correctly led and interpreted the real wishes of the nation. It is, of course, possible that the King may alter his decision at any time in the future, perhaps on the Princess's twenty-first birthday, and grant her some other title, new or old, excluding that of Princess of Wales.

Three Acts of Parliament, widely separated in time, affect, and indeed, control, the constitutional position of the Princess to-day. The first is the Act of Settlement, passed in 1700, in the reign of King William III: the second the Regency Act of 1937, passed at the direct request of the King two months after his accession; and the third, the Act of the same name, passed in 1943, again as a result of a message from His Majesty, delivered to the House of Commons by the Prime Minister. It is a revealing searchlight on the integration of the British monarchy with the British Parliamentary system, that cardinal feature of our democracy which other nations find so difficult to comprehend and even more difficult to imitate successfully, that the position of the Sovereign's daughter should be dependent on votes cast in the elected House with an interval of close on two and a half centuries between them. There are other Acts of Parliament which have a direct effect on members of the Royal House, in particular the Royal Marriages Act of 1772, but these three are the chief in importance.

A very magnificent occasion: Princess Elizabeth arrives at Westminster Abbey for her father's Coronation. Greeting her with a low bow is the Duke of Norfolk, Earl Marshal of England; behind stands her cousin Viscount Lascelles carrying the coronet she will never wear again.

King James the First of "England, Scotland, France, and Ireland", was crowned King of England in 1603 after succeeding to the throne of Scotland as a baby of one year, on July 25 thirty-six years before. His accession paved the way for the Act of Union, joining the two thrones and countries into a single realm under a single Sovereign, in 1706. King James had a daughter, whose name, curiously enough, was also Elizabeth, who married Frederic V, Elector Palatine and King of Bohemia. It was their daughter, the Princess Sophia, who had married the Elector of Hanover, to whom the attention of Parliament was directed when the question of the future succession to the crown became acute at the death of Mary II, the childless wife of William III, in 1694. The widower

A family birthday group on her eighteenth birthday, Princess Elizabeth sits with the King and Queen and Queen Mary. Behind are her uncles and aunts and her sister, the Duke and Duchess of Gloucester, Princess Margaret, the Princess Royal, the Duchess of Kent, and the Earl of Harewood.

King showed no signs of re-marrying, the heiress-presumptive was Princess Anne, and if she died childless—as it proved she did—the line of Protestant succession seemed to be at a full stop. So Parliament, with the assent of King William, passed the Act of Settlement in 1700, setting forth specifically the line of lawful succession to the throne of Great Britain, which, it laid down, was to descend to the Princess Sophia, Electress of Hanover, and "heirs of her body, being protestants". Sophia had died before Queen Anne's death in 1714, and therefore it was her son who became the rightful King of Great Britain, as George I, and who founded the House of Guelph, re-named in 1917, by King George V, as the House of Windsor.

Another provision of the Act of Settlement was that "whosoever shall hereafter come to the possession of this Crown shall join in Communion with the Church of England as by law established".

A custom, whose exact origins seem lost in the remoteness of history, prescribes eighteen as the age at which a Royal person attains majority: but it is majority of a limited kind. Queen Victoria ascended the throne two months after her eighteenth birthday. It was three years before she would, in the ordinary legal sense, leave her minority, yet there was no attempt on the part of anyone to set up, or even to suggest the setting up, of a Regency, as is necessary when a minor succeeds to the throne. She began her reign as a full Queen Regnant, exercising the whole of the Royal powers and prerogatives herself.

On the eve of his eighteenth birthday, King Edward VII, then Prince of Wales, received a letter from his mother informing him that henceforth he must consider himself his own master: and that she would in future offer advice but never obtrude it; thus confirming the idea that the Heir to the Throne comes of age at eighteen.

Accordingly, newspapers proclaimed, as April 21, 1944, approached, that that day would mark the Princess's coming of age. They were only partly right. After the highest legal authorities in the country had, at the King's request, delved deeply into the problem, it emerged that from her eighteenth birthday on, the Princess would automatically become of age, if she ascended the throne, on the exact precedent, of course, of her great-great-grandmother, Queen Victoria. But, if she remained one of the sovereign's subjects, she would not be of age until the normal twenty-one. This position involved an anomaly of a somewhat important kind, affecting the Princess's exercise of Royal functions. The Regency Act of 1937 had made provision for the uninterrupted exercise of the Royal authority during the absence of the Sovereign from his realm, through the medium of Councillors of State, to be empowered by commission of the King through Letters Patent under the Great Seal. But it expressly debarred from those in the line of succession to the Crown who would act as councillors, any who were not "of full age". The Princess, therefore, who might become Queen overnight with full powers, could not take any share in the exercise of the more limited powers entrusted to the Councillors of State during her father's absence abroad. At once, the King took steps to have this matter put right, and sent a message to the Commons by the hand of the Prime Minister, Mr. Churchill, on September 23, 1943, recommending an amendment of the Act to permit the inclusion of the Princess after her eighteenth birthday.

The King's Message, read by Mr. Speaker, included this significant passage:—"The earnest desire of the Queen and myself that our beloved daughter, Princess Elizabeth, should have every opportunity of gaining experience in the duties which would fall upon her in the event of her accession to the throne, leads me to recommend that you should take into consideration the Amendment of the Act mentioned in such manner as to provide for including among the Counsellors of State the person who is heir apparent or heir presumptive to the throne if over the age at which the accession of a sovereign does not necessitate a Regency—namely, the age of eighteen."

At the same time, another anomaly of the 1937 Act was removed, that by which the Queen was automatically included among the Councillors of State, even when, as was the case in the Royal visit to Canada in 1939, she herself was abroad at the time with the King.

It was not long after her birthday that Princess Elizabeth had her first opportunity of exercising the powers newly bestowed on her by Parliament. Immediately before setting out on his flight to Italy, to visit General Sir Harold (now Field Marshal the Viscount) Alexander and his armies, on July 2, the King signed the Warrant under the Great Seal, appointing five Councillors of State who would carry out all Royal functions, except the dissolution of Parliament and the creation of Peers, in his absence. The five were: the Queen, Princess Elizabeth, the Duke of Gloucester, the Princess Royal, and Princess Arthur of Connaught, that is the Consort, and the four next in succession who were of age, of British nationality and domiciled in this country.

The King's nephew, Viscount Lascelles, who had celebrated his twenty-first birthday five months earlier, was compulsorily absent from the country in a German prisoner-of-war camp. His place as the fourth of age in succession was taken by Princess Arthur.

It throws a happy light on the easy intermingling of State duties and normal domestic life in our Royal family that the Princess spent her first day as a Councillor of State

At the start of the holiday which the war interrupted : the Princesses drive with their parents to Crathie Church, near Balmoral, for service on an August Sunday in 1939.

visiting Girl Guides at a camp in Windsor Great Park, with her sister, where they were joined in the afternoon by the Queen.

Her first actual experience of State duties came a day or two later, when, with the Queen, she signed, on behalf of the King, a commission authorizing a Royal Commission, of the Lord Chancellor (Viscount Simon), the Earl of Lucan, and Lord Daryngton, to signify the Royal Assent to Acts just passed. The familiar words, "Signed by the King with his own hand" were replaced at the end of the Commission by the words, "Signed by the Queen and Princess Elizabeth". In the first days of August, with the King still away, Court Circular recorded that the Queen and Princess Elizabeth, "being Councillors of State under His Majesty's Commission, this morning received in audience Major Arthur Young, M.P. (Vice Chamberlain of the Household), who presented an Address from the House of Commons, to which Her Majesty and Her Royal Highness were graciously pleased to make reply on behalf of the King". That was the first occasion on which Court Circular had recorded the Princess as "giving an audience". It will be noted that the Circular spelt the title as "Councillors" whereas the Parliamentary usage is the archaic form "Counsellors". Next day, in similiar terms, it was announced that the Queen and the Princess had received an address from the House of Lords, presented by the Lord Chamberlain (the Earl of Clarendon), to which they also made reply on behalf of the King.

The Councillors of State are vested with the full Royal powers and prerogatives, with two important exceptions: they may neither dissolve Parliament, nor may they create peers. These two powers are reserved for the exclusive use of the sovereign himself, since they are the two most potentially important instruments of government still

The Princess's personal standard flies from the yard-arm of H.M.S. Superb : note the white "cadency label" across the top.

pertaining to the Crown. Any one Councillor's signature on a State document carries the full weight of the deputed authority of the King, though in practice, it is customary for two to sign, as did the Queen and Princess Elizabeth in the instance cited above.

Since then, Princess Elizabeth has had no further opportunity of exercising any active part in the affairs of State, and during the King's forthcoming absence from the realm, in his other realm of South Africa, she will be with her father and mother, so that neither the Queen nor the Heiress Presumptive will be able to act as councillors for His Majesty on this occasion.

Nor has the Princess, so far, been appointed to "His Majesty's Most Honorable Privy Council", that ancient and still most powerful body, not elected by the people, but chosen by the King, whose origins go back to the "Curia Regis" of pre-Norman times, and whose dictates, the well-known "Orders in Council", ruled, under the Parliamentary authority of the Emergency Powers Defence Act, the daily lives of all the King's subjects during the war. There are precedents in plenty for the appointment of a woman Privy Councillor: several are among the three hundred odd members to-day. An heir-apparent has nearly always been made a Privy Councillor and it is reasonable to assume that the Princess will be sworn in as a Councillor some time in the future, though not necessarily, as might be thought, on her twenty-first birthday.

The King's daughter is a Princess of the Blood Royal, but not a peeress in her own right, which would seem to remove her from the disability attaching to peers of the realm, who are expressly debarred from the franchise. Whether she becomes entitled to the vote on reaching twenty-one is a nice question for the constitutional lawyers: but it is extremely unlikely that she would ever use it. Should the King confer a peerage on his daughter at any time, and should the existing bar on women who are peeresses taking part in the debates of the House of Lords be raised, there would be no reason why Princess Elizabeth should not become the first woman to take her seat in the Lords, but that is carrying the question into speculative realms.

Since pre-Restoration days, the reigning sovereign has been excluded from the House of Commons in session, a right so jealously guarded by the "faithful Commons" that they take the trouble to shut and bar the door of their chamber in the face of Black Rod, the King's Messenger, when he comes to summon them to the other House to hear the King's Speech at the opening of Parliament. But the ban does not extend to the King's heir, who may listen to the Common debates as often as he—or she—may wish, and significantly, in the plans for the new House that is to arise from the bombed and burned ruins of the old, provision has been made for a private lift for Princess Elizabeth to take her to her special seat in the gallery, whenever she wants to hear what the M.P.s are saying. Up to now, she has not availed herself of her privilege, though she has been to Parliament—on May 17, 1945, when she heard both Houses tender their congratulations to her father on the victory in Europe. That, of course, was a formal occasion, but the Princess follows the give-and-take of political debates with much closer attention than even most M.P.s suspect, reading them fully in Hansard, the official report of the debates, which is sent her at the Palace daily while the House is in session.

The Coat of Arms

THE COAT OF ARMS granted by the King to Princess Elizabeth on her eighteenth birthday was designed by Sir Gerald Wollaston as his last task before retiring from the post of Garter King of Arms, the supreme arbiter of British armorial bearings. It consists of the Royal arms, "differenced", in the heraldic term, "with a cadency label of devices" indicating her position as daughter of the sovereign, or "cadet" of the Royal House of Windsor.

The label of three points is in argent, the centre point charged with the Tudor Rose, and each of the other two with the Cross of St. George. These devices were chosen by the King, in accordance with the ancient rules of coat-armour, unchanged since the days of Crecy when visored knights had no means of identifying friend or foe save by their blazoned shields. The white Tudor Rose of York, not previously used for such a purpose, was chosen in allusion to the fact that, before his accession he was Duke, and his daughter Princess Elizabeth, of York. The labels are charged at the top centre of the shield, and repeated on the shoulders of the lion and unicorn supporters.

The Princess has not yet adopted a motto of her own.

On her personal standard, Princess Elizabeth has the same label of argent charged across the upper quarters of the Royal Arms.

Princess Margaret's coat of arms, approved by the King at the same time as her sister's, differs in that the three-pointed label is charged in the centre with the thistle, indicating her birth in Scotland. The two other points are charged with the Tudor Rose, to indicate, as in the case of her sister, her first rank as a Princess of York.

The Princess's personal standard, which she is entitled to fly, as a person of Royal rank, over any dwelling where she is in residence (except when there is a senior-ranking member of the Royal family there as well) is, like her coat of arms, a relic of the days of high chivalry, when the Sovereign and the great Princes under him in battle, displayed their standards to be a rallying point for their men-at-arms. The sight of the standard flying through the haze and dust of battle was proof that the King was present in person, and was a ready means of identifying the Royal quarters for those who had urgent business with him.

Such usages seem mere romantic dreams in these more prosaic times when sovereigns no longer ride into battle at the head of their men. But in fact, Princess Elizabeth's standard has served a like useful purpose of identification many times in recent months.

On her visits to provincial towns, she drives not in the easily recognised maroon and scarlet Royal cars, but in a plain black saloon that would be difficult to distinguish from other cars in the procession except that from its radiator top there flies a small flag, coloured predominantly red and yellow, which is the Princess's standard in miniature. Without it, many in the waiting crowds would miss seeing the Princess completely.

The Princess's standard has flown several times over Buckingham Palace when she has been there alone in the absence of the King and Queen, but most passers-by, glancing casually up at the forty-foot flagstaff on the Palace roof, have not recognised it, missing the white cadency label, and taking it for the Royal Standard itself.

The colour photograph opposite is of the actual parchment warrant, bearing the original grant of arms. It was taken by special permission at the College of Arms, where the design was executed in 1944.

The Princess's Coat of Arms: photographed in colour by special permission from the original parchment grant at the College of Arms

Photograph: Fox Photos Ltd.

CHAPTER FOUR

The Unknown Princess

HER EARLY SECLUSION AND HOW SHE EMERGED FROM IT

FOR the first fourteen or fifteen years of her life, Princess Elizabeth lived, as far as the general public were concerned, in almost complete seclusion. This was, as has already been indicated, a result of the deliberate policy laid down by her parents, and fully approved by King George and Queen Mary, at the time of her birth. Nothing would have been easier or on the surface more beneficial to the monarchy than to yield to the popular clamour for more public appearances by the Princess, already christened "the Nation's Darling", and a series of functions attended by her as a little girl would undoubtedly have set loose a great wave of loyal, if sentimental, enthusiasm, for the Royal family as a whole. But such a move was far from the thoughts of her father and mother. Instead, they wished to shield their daughter for as long as possible from the fierce glare of publicity that must, as they well knew, one day be turned upon her. Each and every request for the Princess's attendance at functions, no matter of what kind, no matter how worthy the cause for which they were being held, was turned down with a politely worded but firm refusal. No amount of persuasion, no inducement could be made to affect this attitude. Recognising the right of the public at home, and in the Empire overseas, to know something of how the Princess was growing up, the Duke and Duchess permitted a certain small number of authorised, official studio portraits of her on her birthdays and on other exceptional occasions, to be reproduced in the Press. But that was all. Once the first full spate of interest in her as a baby had passed, the Duke and Duchess took good care that, wherever the Princess was, at 145, Piccadilly, at Royal Lodge, Windsor, at Glamis Castle, at St. Paul's Walden, at Sandringham or at Balmoral, she should be protected from all intruders on her privacy. The occasional unauthorised pictures, and even more the often wildly inaccurate gossip paragraphs about her that from time to time appeared, caused the Duke and Duchess nothing but annoyance.

This policy had the natural, though unlooked for, effect of stimulating public desire to know more about the little Princess, and all sorts of stratagems were evolved by the more determined and less scrupulous newspapers to satisfy it.

Stories half founded on truth, stories with no truth at all, were repeated in private houses, and found their way into some newspapers, until, by the time the Princess was only a few years old, a regular apocrypha had grown up around her. Some of these legends—for they were nothing more—persisted for many years, in spite of any number of official denials. One excellent story which first gained currency when Elizabeth was about ten years old, told how, each year, her father gave her as a birthday present a single pearl, growing in size as she grew up, so that, by the time she would be twenty-one, she would own a beautiful necklace of twenty-one perfectly graded pearls. So charming did that story seem that it has lasted until to-day, and was repeated verbatim on the Princess's twentieth birthday. The story certainly has charm and excellence—but is

E

An early visit to Westminster Abbey. Princess Elizabeth walking with her grandparents as King George and Queen Mary attend a service for the unemployed in 1934.

completely untrue. The King did not at any time, either at her birth, or when she was ten, begin such a practice, and the double string of pearls which Princess Elizabeth so frequently wears to-day were a gift not from her father, but from her grandfather and grandmother, King George V and Queen Mary, at the time of their Silver Jubilee.

Another, and less apocryphal, story of the Princess's very young days both illustrates how she was early taught the importance of good manners, and shows her natural keen wits. When she was five, she had been rude one day to her governess. As punishment, it was decreed she should be "sent to Coventry" till she had apologised. Next morning, when lesson time came, Princess Elizabeth greeted Miss Crawford with her usual smiling "Good morning". There was no answer. Princess Elizabeth tried again, with a similar result. When there was no response to her third "Good morning", the Princess determined on stern measures. "Good morning," she said once again, adding this time the imperative words, "It's Royalty speaking!" When her mother heard the story, she explained that Royalty was not an excuse for bad, but carries an obligation to exceptionally good, manners, and the Princess remembered the lesson.

She also remembered the trick for attracting attention. A year or so later, she visited an agricultural show in the country with Queen Mary, who had requested in advance that the show people should not keep the little Princess talking too long. When she asked an old countryman exhibitor about his cattle, the old man, with Queen Mary's admonition

An informal picture that shows the close resemblance between the King and his daughter: taken just before the King and Queen left for Canada in 1939.

in his mind, refused to be drawn into conversation. The Princess repeated her questions. Still there was silence. Then Princess Elizabeth decided to apply pressure. "You must answer, you know," she told the old man. "It's Royalty asking."

Another lesson of those early days which has often to stand her in good stead nowadays was to suffer boredom without showing it. This is one of the polite usages in which Royalty has perforce to be expert. Self-important local figures do not always consider the feelings of their Royal visitors when declaiming long and platitudinous speeches, but never by the movement of a muscle will Princess Elizabeth show her feelings, however impatient she may well be to proceed with her programme. It was when callers came to visit the Duchess of York at Piccadilly that the Princess had her first lessons in this difficult art. If she happened to be downstairs when the visitors arrived, she saw how her parents received them with courtesy, took her cue from them, and thus learned her first lessons in good manners. She had her natural likes and dislikes among the "grown-ups" some of whom were very boring to her childish mind, especially when their arrival chanced to interrupt some game or other, but it was in this way that she began to learn self-restraint and consideration for others, both of which qualities she possesses in a marked degree to-day.

It was in those nursery days, too, that she learned of the eager public interest in all her activities, in her private as well as her official life, which makes her so eager and so grateful for a little privacy and freedom from intrusion to-day.

QUEEN OF TO-MORROW

Photographers in those days would conceal themselves at vantage points along the route they thought the Princess would follow when she went out for a walk, a drive, or a ride. Servants and members of the Duke and Duchess's household were bombarded by questions, but all in vain. The stratagems were met by counter-stratagems, the questions by complete unrevealing silence, until at last it became recognised, even by the most persistent, that the Princess was not to be made into a public figure yet awhile, that her childhood and girlhood were not to be spoilt by outside prying.

So well and successfully was this wise policy carried out that it was possible for the Princess and her sister—for, after the birth of Princess Margaret, exactly the same policy of privacy was pursued in her case—not only to lead normal lives but even occasionally to make one of their rare appearances in public without being recognised. At such functions as the Military Tournament at Olympia, where they sat in the Royal Box, or on great occasions of State, at the Coronation, at the return of the King and Queen from their Canadian tour, the Princesses were, of course, recognised, and given a particularly enthusiastic welcome by the crowds. But on other occasions, where they were not expected to be present, their attendance often passed unnoticed.

It was while the King and Queen were in Canada and the United States that this aspect of affairs became specially noticeable: and there was nothing that could have given more pleasure to their parents than to hear from Queen Mary, and from Miss Crawford, in their frequent, detailed letters reporting the Princesses' activities, that they were escaping over much attention from the public.

At this time, Queen Mary, much to her own pleasure, and to the delight of her granddaughters, began to escort them on the series of visits to museums and places of historic interest mentioned in a previous chapter, and these visits inevitably meant that the Princesses were seen by more people than ever before. Queen Mary, with her characteristic consideration for others, refused to allow the public to be excluded from the galleries or museums where she was taking her granddaughters. All she stipulated was that there should be no advance announcement made to attract large crowds. People who were visiting a museum for their own pleasure or instruction, by chance at the same time as the Princesses, should not, she felt, be deprived of the opportunity of seeing them, so long as crowds of sightseers did not flock in, merely because they were there. And the surprising thing was that, at a number of these places, not only did the sightseers not crowd in, but most of the people already in the buildings failed to notice the Royal party at all.

This phenomenon was particularly marked on the day when the Princesses had the great thrill of riding in an ordinary underground train for the first time in either of their lives. Lady Helen Graham, Lady-in-Waiting to the Queen, and Miss Crawford accompanied the two Princesses, when they drove up to the imposing entrance to St. James's Park Station, headquarters of the London Passenger Transport Board, where Epstein's queer statues of Night and Morning keep watch over London's hurrying millions. No highly placed representatives of the Board were there to greet them. That would have spoilt the whole thing, by turning it into an official occasion, which was just what it was designed not to be. Instead, the Lady-in-Waiting took the four tickets, while the Princesses —then aged twelve and eight respectively—watched in wonderment as the change and the tickets appeared as if by magic, the party passed through the turnstiles, unrecognised by the busy ticket collector, who afterwards almost refused to believe that he had really

Waving goodbye to the King and Queen as they leave Portsmouth for Canada in 1939. It was months before the Princesses saw their parents again.

Princess Elizabeth acknowledges the greeting of the crowd from the Palace balcony on her grandfather's Silver Jubilee Day. King George V wears the white silk shoulder ribbons of the Collar of his Order.

seen the Princesses, and down onto the platform to await the next east-bound train. To the Princesses, it was a really exciting adventure. Everything was new to them, the advertisements on the walls, the tobacco and newspaper kiosks, the changing names on the train indicators, the bustle of passengers surging in and out of the lighted coaches, the loud voices of the porters calling the names of stations. They looked about them in wonder, asking Lady Helen quick, eager questions. It was perhaps two or three minutes before the right train came in, but in that time no one noticed the little Royal group standing on the platform. Glancing at them, a good many passers-by probably thought "How like Princess Elizabeth that girl is", never imagining that it could possibly be the Princess herself on the underground station.

In the inner circle train, it was just the same. No special seats had been reserved for the Royal travellers. They sat demurely enough with their two ladies, in a third-class carriage, among other passengers, looking up at the underground maps, following the progress of the all-too-short journey, peering out of the windows as the train ran into Westminster and then Charing Cross. Here came another thrill, their first ride on an escalator, as they were led through the maze of passages and stairs to change into the Northern line for Tottenham Court Road station, where their destination was the Young Women's Christian Association headquarters in Great Russell Street. Princess Elizabeth stepped gaily and confidently onto the moving stairway, with her left foot correctly first, then turned to watch her sister, as Princess Margaret, following not quite so confidently, stepped on with wrong foot first, but quickly recovered her balance. As the Princesses with their attendant ladies went slowly down the escalator, hundreds of Londoners being borne upwards on the opposite moving staircase looked in surprise at the two demure girls, in simply cut coats and tam-o'-shanters, puzzling to know whether they could really be the King's daughters.

Not to be recognised was an added delight to the Princesses, both of whom were already familiar with their Arabian Nights and the incognito journeyings of Haroun-al-Raschid. To any ordinary child, to spend a day as a Princess would be a fairy story come true: and to a Princess, to be treated, and to be able to behave, for a few hours as an ordinary child, is almost equally a magical experience.

In the brightly-lit tube carriage, the Princesses again amused themselves reading the station names and checking the progress of their journey—just as nearly every child does on its first underground journey. At Tottenham Court Road, the little Royal party hurried off the train and up the stairs, leaving behind them some very perplexed passengers, who went on scratching their heads and arguing if their fellow travellers had been the Princesses or not, till the question was settled by a paragraph in the morning papers, announcing that the Royal sisters had been for their first tube ride.

After a visit to the "help-yourself" cafeteria of the YWCA, where they took cups of tea, the Princesses set out on the return journey to the Palace, descending again into the Tube station, taking tickets, changing at Charing Cross, and so arriving at St. James's Park again, where the big Royal car was waiting to take them across to Buckingham Palace. This time, things did not go quite so well. Princess Margaret, who had firmly refused to be separated from the tickets throughout the exciting journey, forgot all about such formalities as handing them over at the end of it, with the result that the ticket collector had to run out into the street and ask the small passenger for them. Then he, if no one else, was in the secret. When he returned to his post at the platform barrier, he proudly announced the identity of the ticket holders, adding that he would ask the Board permission to keep the tickets as a souvenir.

Back at the Palace, the Princesses wrote a full account of their adventures in their next letter to the King and Queen in Canada, adding, according to report at the time, a petition to be allowed soon to make their first ride in a London bus. That request, if it was ever made, was not, apparently, granted. It was not until July, 1946, that the

In the grounds of Buckingham Palace in Coronation Year: a happy family group.

Princesses made their first bus ride, paying fares as ordinary passengers on a country service from Dartmouth.

After that brief period of unexpected and unannounced visits to public places, including the Children's Corner at the Zoo, which passed away their spare time while their father and mother were in Canada, the Princesses reverted to their normal life of seclusion, disappearing entirely from the public gaze in August of that fateful year, 1939, when they went north to Balmoral with the King and Queen for the Court's summer stay in the Highlands, which, this year, was to be so quickly and suddenly interrupted by war, though they themselves would stay longer in Scotland than either of them ever imagined.

QUEEN OF TO-MORROW

A wartime river trip: with the Queen and Princess Margaret, she accompanies the King on an inspection of the Thames Home Guard in 1940.

Princess Elizabeth was thirteen when war broke out. For another three full years, she remained out of the public gaze, continuing with her studies, her home interests, and her training, until, at sixteen, she began to emerge into the limelight. It was a gradual, carefully regulated process, so that of no single moment can it be said it was then that the Princess became a public figure. She was introduced by degrees into the fierce light (and the photographers' flashlamps) that beat on the faces of the famous. So skilfully was the transformation of the Princess-stay-at-home into Princess Elizabeth, the public figure, effected that not only were the people of the Empire prepared gently for her emergence, and given time to assess her before she took full place as Heiress to the Throne, but she herself was almost unaware of the tremendous change that was slowly but surely taking place in her life, a fact that may well account in great measure for her composure and easy presence in public to-day. As the veil was lifted more and more, first by the Princess appearing with the King and Queen at private and semi-private functions at Windsor (for example, the weekly film shows at the Castle, to which troops from the neighbourhood were invited), then by her making more public appearances at ceremonies at which she was herself the central figure, and the public began to know her better, she began to fill an increasing place in the public mind and affections. Requests for her attendance at all sorts of functions, possible and impossible, began to pour into the Palace. More than once, on visits to dockyards and war factories, the King and Queen heard, to their private delight, mingled with the cheers and applause, shouts from the men—and especially from the women—war-workers, "Why didn't you bring the Princess? We want to see Elizabeth!"

THE UNKNOWN PRINCESS

But the question of the Princess's first official public tour was one not lightly to be settled. All kinds of considerations had to be taken into account. There had been repeated requests from all parts of the country to see her, there were many claims and counter-claims to be weighed against each other. From Scotland came strong pleas that as the daughter of the King of Scotland as well as of the King of England, and of a Scottish mother, into the bargain, the Princess should undoubtedly make her first appearance north of the Tweed. That claim was carefully weighed along with the others, but finally the King decided that the honour must go to Wales, thus fostering in a new way the ancient ties that bind the now Prince-less Principality to the throne.

Princesses do not, in the accepted sense, "come out". They do not make their début by being "presented" at Court. But the year in which her friends would be making their first curtseys in the Throne Room of Buckingham Palace, would normally be, for the heiress to the Throne, a year of crowded gaiety and entertainment, of glittering ceremonial and pomp, of theatre parties, opera visits, dances, State balls, of fashionable race meetings, picnics, horse-shows, and other social occasions of greater or less import.

Princess Elizabeth had none of this in her "débutante" year, when she was eighteen.

Instead of a background of Royal splendour, with the soft lights of the rose-crystal chandeliers in the Palace ballroom gleaming on uniforms of red, blue and gold, with exquisitely dressed and jewelled women moving gracefully through the throng, and the murmur of small-talk blending with the subdued music of a string band, she made her début in much grimmer, more realistic surroundings.

At the piano : the Royal sisters learned early to play duets together.

"Look at the soldiers" Princess Elizabeth enjoys the Trooping of the Colour parade on her grandfather's birthday.

QUEEN OF TO-MORROW

It was the vivid yellow glare of metal foundry furnaces that lit up her face in a harsh, metallic light, the deep rumble of the rolling mills that drowned her words as she met her father's subjects for the first time. In place of the white and gold walls of the Palace, she saw the high drab walls of a great metal plant, with their blacked-out windows and urgent placards begging for greater and greater efforts for war.

That was how this Princess of the twentieth century first came to the people, in the big tin-plate mills near Newport, Monmouthshire, where wiry Welsh metal workers, sweating in the hot air of the furnaces, greeted her with grins of pleasure, and cheers that could scarce be heard above the noise of the never-stopping machinery. It was a strange, moving experience the Princess will never forget.

Deliberately, and surely with great wisdom, the King had chosen this setting for the opening of his daughter's public life. No King of England has ever had a greater, deeper or more intimate knowledge of industrial Britain than King George VI. As a young Prince, he took up the study of industry and industrial conditions, then an almost despised subject, of no interest to the world of fashion; acquired, in a long series of painstaking factory visits all over the country, that attracted little public attention, a vast stock of knowledge of production methods, trade customs, relations between employers, managers, and workers, and welfare schemes: and became known for his serious, purposeful interest in all industrial problems. On this solid foundation, the King went on to build up a great knowledge of the new methods of mass-production in wartime, and a valuable familiarity with the point of view of the men—and women—behind the lathes and tools and at the benches, as with the Queen he made his tireless tours of war factories and production centres. Now, when it was time for Princess Elizabeth to enter her public life the King could conceive of no better start for her than to go at once to a big works, vital to the country alike in war as in peace, and see for herself modern industry in being.

A little over-awed by the novelty of this strange fantastic world like nothing she had ever seen before, the Princess stood, in those first few moments by the furnaces, silent and absorbed, watching the quick, skilful movements of the men as they tended the swirling bubbling metal released from the foundries. Silent, too, the King, his blue-and-gold uniform as an Admiral of the Fleet turned to a queer purple and silver in the furnace glare, watched his daughter, while the foundry men, unconscious of the moment of history they were sharing, went on with their job, stopping only to throw quick appraising glances at their Royal watchers.

From that first significant factory visit, the Princess went on with her parents to other centres of war production in South Wales, to the mining valleys, the docks of Swansea, the Treforest Trading Estate, where three miles of cheering people greeted the Royal party with waving Union Jacks and the Dragon flag of Wales, and everywhere there was a special warmth in the cheers for the Princess. For eighteen years the Welsh people had waited to see the daughter of the Royal House, and what was originally designed mainly as another of the many Royal wartime factory tours was turned into a two-day progress of triumph for Princess Elizabeth. Miners, factory girls, housewives, dockers— a whole cross-section of the people of Wales-at-war turned out in thousands to see her. All through the busy two-day tour, with every minute of the day taken up in the rapid non-stop style of the King's war tours, Princess Elizabeth remained her calm, collected self, walking always a little behind her mother and father, watching from the background

A lucky dip in fancy dress: at a children's party given by Viscountess Astor

as they talked to war-workers, men and women of the Civil Defence services at parades, and the regional and civic leaders of the country at official luncheons and receptions. As the Royal car drove from town to town, slowing nearly to walking pace through the crowds, the Princess sat in front of the King and Queen, smiling her thanks and acknowledging the cheers with slight bows. At several points, U.S. soldiers were in the front of the crowds, cheering as loudly as any. In several factories, she lingered alone to exchange a few words with girls of her own age whom she saw at the benches and the lathes. At one, she accepted with shy grace the bouquet proffered her by a girl charge-hand, who told the Princess that every girl in her section had subscribed towards it. And she did it all with such unaffected charm that the persistent Welsh, unable to hail her officially with the titles of the Principality, bestowed on her the unofficial title of "Ein Tywysoges"—"Our own Princess". At the end of the strenuous two days, the Princess seemed as fresh and unfatigued as at the beginning, and when the Royal train, on which she and the King and Queen had spent the two nights of their stay, steamed out on its journey back to London, Wales indeed was the Princess's. She had won all hearts.

Wales was again honoured a year later, when the Princess went to Cardiff to fulfil her first engagements alone out of London. The welcome she had at the City Hall in Cardiff when, wearing uniform as Commodore of the Sea Rangers, she arrived to attend the Council meeting of the Girl Guides Association for Wales, showed that the Welsh love for her had increased with the passing months. That night, after the formal proceedings of the Council were over, the Princess relaxed with two hundred Girl Guides in camp on a hillside near Cardiff. Sitting round the camp fire with them, she joined in singing the camp songs, laughing at her own failure to keep up with the action songs, entering into the camp spirit just as her father used to do at his Industrial and Public School Boys camps before the war, and ate with zest a camp supper of soup, stewed meat and trifle.

It was when she was eighteen that Princess Elizabeth made her first speech in public, at the annual meeting of the Court of Governors of the Queen Elizabeth Hospital for Children, Hackney, of which she had just been elected President.

Six days after her eighteenth birthday, Princess Victoria, too, made her first public speech. But the setting and the occasion were very different.

In accordance with the ponderous custom of the day, the Lord Mayor of London went in state from Guildhall with other civic dignitaries to Kensington Palace to present congratulatory addresses to the Princess and her mother, the Duchess of Kent. After the Duchess had replied in stilted, stylised phrases, Princess Victoria spoke, in reply to the address to herself. She uttered one sentence: "I am very thankful for all your kindness, and my mother has expressed all my feelings."

The same note of genuine simplicity and sincerity rings in those few words as in the first public speech of Princess Elizabeth, more than a century later. But the modern Princess spoke for herself. Her audience of charitably-minded hospital patrons, one or two of her own older friends among them, was perhaps less awe-inspiring than the robed City Fathers who waited on the young Victoria. But she was alone, far from the familiar surroundings of her own home. The blaze of cinema lights dazzled her eyes, the whirring of recording cameras sounded in her ears as she rose to speak.

As Commodore of the Sea Rangers, Princess Elizabeth addresses the Council of the Girl Guides Association for Wales in the Temple of Peace at Cardiff.

Her first public speech. The Princess addresses the Board of the Queen Elizabeth Hospital for Children, Hackney, as its new President. Lord Iliffe, the retiring President, is at her side.

Here is the text of that, the first of the many hundreds of speeches she will be called upon to make as the years go by.

Written in advance, it bears the authentic stamp of the Princess's own phrasing, but to appreciate the proper worth of these few sentences, it is necessary to have heard the young Princess utter them in her charming, clear and well-rounded voice, to have seen her glance a little nervously round the crowded board room of the Hospital, flooded with the over-powering glare of the cinema lights (which she did not expect to be there), shrug her shoulders, make a little *moue*, then read her speech almost as easily as if she were still in her own quiet room at the Palace, rehearsing it.

The Princess said: "Lord Iliffe, Ladies and Gentlemen, I should like first to thank you all very sincerely for the kind welcome you have given me to-day as your new President —and especially Lord Iliffe and Sir Hill Child for what they have just said in proposing my election.

"I need not say how proud I am to be associated with the Hospital in this way. I feel that I have long had very close ties with it. It bears my mother's name and my father, as Lord Iliffe reminded us, was himself President of the Queen's Hospital for many years. He was deeply interested and, indeed, one of my earliest recollections was hearing him talk of it, and of the wonderful work it was doing for children.

"I shall always endeavour to do all I can to help in the continuance of that work in the great institution which has emerged from the amalgamation of the two Hospitals. I know well how deeply interested in it are all of you who are here to-day, and what splendid service you and others are giving to it in its widespread activities. As the first act of my presidency, I should like to assure you that my own interest, and my own service, will always be given just as wholeheartedly to what we all know to be a great cause."

THE UNKNOWN PRINCESS

Simply-worded, forthright, and unpretentious, the speech obeyed the first law of all good oratory. It exactly fitted the occasion. A point that charmed the Princess's hearers was that she did not once use the formal expression of "the King and Queen", but referred to Their Majesties simply and naturally as "my mother and my father". That family note, recurring frequently in Princess Elizabeth's subsequent speeches, never fails to stimulate applause. The simple homely words ring true, warm and true, opening for a moment a window into the happy family life of the British monarchy, with an effect that the cold terms of the Royal titles could never have. Once, on an occasion of much greater significance, later on in the Princess's career as a speaker, she was called upon to make the main speech of the day at a ceremony of great national importance. This time, the speech had been carefully prepared for her, for much of what she had to say referred to technical matters of which she had little knowledge. It was a long speech, and, of necessity, rather devoid of human interest. Going over it beforehand, the Princess decided on two minor-seeming, but important, alterations. Instead of using the formal phrase, "Mr. Chairman" at the opening, she substituted the name of the gentleman concerned, making the whole speech sound more personal. Then at the end, in a reference to the fact that the King, as a qualified Service pilot—he passed his tests in the early days of the R.A.F. at the end of the 1914–18 war—wears the winged badge of the Fleet Air Arm pilots on the sleeve of his Admiral's uniform, the original draft had the phrase "His Majesty the King". When she came to this point, the Princess said merely "My father"—and her audience, up to then a little apathetic, broke into cheers and clapped at the human touch.

As a general rule, the Princess prepares all her speeches herself, taking a real pleasure in the phrasing and construction. If it is on a subject near to her own interests that she is to speak, on music or literature or child welfare, she will often not even need the aid of notes from outside. But if it is a new subject that is unfamiliar to her, she asks for draft notes for guidance, so that she may be accurate in reference to facts and figures, then uses these as the bare bricks with which to construct her own speech. Nearly always, up to now, the Princess has spoken from notes. It is almost an unwritten law in the Royal family not to make extempory speeches, since Royal sayings, if not carefully thought out, might easily be subject afterwards to misconstruction. But with the help of a first-class memory, she can—and does—"read" her speeches with only occasional glances at the manuscript, thus giving, as experienced Parliamentary orators well know, the effect of spontaneity and freshness, and adding greatly to the lively interest of the speech. Now and then it happens that there is an unexpected call for a speech which cannot possibly be prepared in advance. When this happens the Princess is always equal to the occasion. With perhaps only two or three short sentences, spoken easily and with sincerity, she meets the demand, and charms the hearts of her hearers, where a long speech in stilted phrases, or a short one spoken with hesitation would be equally wrong. That is an ability which sounds easy to acquire, but is not, especially for one accustomed to speaking from manuscript—as again a good many M.P.s could testify!

The Princess's prose style, as reflected in her speeches, is direct, free from affectation and innocent of florid imagery and phrasing. She has read extensively most of the great masters of public speaking, from Demosthenes to Burke, listened to, or read, all the great war speeches of Winston Churchill and President Roosevelt, and, in addition, has as

The Princess talks to an Ulster Brownie: at Londonderry on her first visit to Northern Ireland

a background her extensive reading of the great classic English writers, which, with a natural gift for clear expression, enables her to say what she wishes, crisply and clearly, without waste of words. And, no matter what the occasion, whether it be the launch of a great ship, or merely a meeting of the Girl Guides, she takes equal care and trouble over her speech, both in preparing it and delivering it.

Her first speech in public, her visit to Wales with her parents, marked the end of her seclusion. Those sequestered days were gone, and the more the people saw of her, the more popular did she become. Scotland had its first official sight of the Princess six months after Wales, when, accompanying the King and Queen on their way south from Balmoral, she spent two days in Edinburgh, visiting Service clubs, schools and factories. If the Scots welcome was a trifle more staid than the Welsh, in keeping with the more reserved national character, it was none the less enthusiastic and sincere for that, and there have never been more full-throated cheers in the Scottish capital than when she drove for the first time alone through the tall iron gates of Holyroodhouse on her way to receive purses from the Scottish Y.W.C.A. at the Assembly Hall.

Ulster, as eager as Wales or Scotland to greet the heiress to the throne, had to wait to see her until 1945, when she came with the King and Queen on their victory visit to Northern Ireland. This time, at the last moment, plans for a sea crossing had to be abandoned, and the Princess made her entry into Northern Ireland by air. It was her first flight, and the first time that a British sovereign, his consort and his heir, had travelled together by plane.

They made the flight together in a single plane, an arrangement that would have shocked the timid Ministers of an earlier day, who even felt compelled to venture a mild protest to Queen Victoria at the proposal to send both sons of the Prince of Wales together on a cruise in the *Ophir* on the score of danger to the security of the succession!

A silver-bodied Dakota aircraft, guarded by two squadrons of Mustang fighters from a Polish R.A.F. wing, four Stirling bombers, and two Warwick aircraft of the air sea-rescue service, carried the Royal passengers, and the Princess, in her A.T.S. uniform, left no doubt in the minds of anyone at Long Kesh Aerodrome, where the two hour flight from Northolt ended, that she had enjoyed every minute of the trip. Next day, with the shouts and cheers of the Ulster loyalists ringing in her ears, the Princess went to Stormont, where the King opened the new session of the Ulster Parliament. In the Commons Chamber—used for the day by the Senate—she left her parents, to sit in the gallery beside the Speaker's Chair and watch, but take no part in, the elaborate ceremonial of the Royal opening.

Five thousand war workers met the King and Queen and the Princess at a party in the Botanic Gardens, and it is no disrespect to the King and Queen to say that Princess Elizabeth was the main centre of interest to most of those present. She left the party to attend alone an informal reception for members of the three women's services—an instance of the gradualness with which the Princess has so successfully been brought into public life, first merely accompanying the King and Queen to various engagements, then carrying out a single engagement on her own in the midst of a visit by them, and finally, going about the country on her own.

The record of Princess Elizabeth's public engagements since her eighteenth birthday clearly demonstrates this gradual development of her life in public. From April 21, 1944, till the end of the year, her appearance alone in public without her parents numbered eight: in 1945, the number rose to thirty: and that same number had been reached long before 1946 had half run its course: sometimes at the rate of four in a week, with youth parades and services nearly every weekend. Many of these engagements were—and many of her future ones will also be—"first visits" to different parts of the country, first experiences of various kinds, but already it is possible to detect a pattern in Princess Elizabeth's public activities which gives several clues to her character.

Each year, in May, one afternoon is set aside to attend the annual court of governors of the Queen Elizabeth Hospital for Children, Hackney; another is booked for the annual meeting of the National Society for the Prevention of Cruelty to Children—the Princess is President of both bodies. The autumn concert and prizegiving of the Royal College of Music is another regular item on her yearly list of engagements. Again, she is President of the College, which was, indeed, the very first adult public position which the King allowed her to take up, by reason of her own great and abiding interest in music, as, on her twelfth birthday, he had allowed her to be made President of the Children's League of the Princess Elizabeth of York Hospital for Children at Shadwell, now a component member of the general Queen Elizabeth Hospital for Children.

A.T.S. passing-out parades, youth organisations, especially the Girl Guides, occur frequently in the lists of her engagements. When civic authorities approach her with plans for a visit, she insists that local contingents of all the young people's organisations shall, as far as possible, be included in the programme. When there is any question of preference for the choice of a guard of honour, or other special duty near her, it is the Girl Guides who get the Princess's vote: for they were her own organisation as a girl.

Thus Princess Elizabeth in her public life shows two of the outstanding qualities of her personality, loyalty and steadfastness. She is not, and never has been, a person who takes up interests lightly, only to drop them just as easily a few weeks later. If and when her interest is aroused, she goes into whatever subject it is with thoroughness and application: and her interest is not allowed to wane with the passing of time or the claims of other new matters on her attention. To do this successfully requires a keen and retentive mind, and an ability to dispose well of time, both of which accomplishments Princess Elizabeth has already shown she possesses in so marked a degree as to bring the figure of her never-hurried, always interested, widely and deeply read grandmother, Queen Mary, vividly to mind.

To Queen Mary it has fallen to take charge of a recent, and important, new aspect

At the start of her first flight : the Princess follows the King aboard a silver Dakota aircraft at Northolt to leave for Northern Ireland.

With her mother, watching a display by girls of the National Fire Service at the N.F.S. headquarters at Lambeth.

of the Princess's public activities, her increasingly frequent visits to factories, particularly those where a great percentage of the workers are women. These visits, unquestionably, afford splendid opportunities for contact between the Princess and her future subjects which would be difficult, if not impossible, to arrange otherwise. They are the outcome of plans made for the Princess by the King, prompted by recollections of the invaluable apprenticeship to industrial knowledge he served himself when factory visits as President of the Industrial Welfare Society occupied so much of his time as Duke of York. Like those early visits of the King's, soon after the Great War, the Princess's visits to factories are, with set purpose, run on workaday lines, with a minimum of formality. Red carpets *do* tend to appear on stairways, flowers are apt to be massed at entrances, floors, walls and benches are at their cleanest and tidiest, but the work of the factory goes on without interruption—or at least with no more interruption than is caused by natural curiosity— while the Princess is there, for the whole idea is for her to see things as they are in everyday guise, and not to be shown a series of idealised set-pieces. Indeed, for her own part, there is no doubt the Princess would prefer all formalities and red carpets to be done away with on these occasions, though she realises that in practice that is asking the impossible.

The first of these visits was to a big modern stocking factory at Baldock: the next to the giant Battersea power station whose twin towers dominate the skyline to the south-west if you look—as Princess Elizabeth has often looked—at London's vastness from the roof of Buckingham Palace; the third to the General Electric Company's research laboratories at Wembley; and many others will follow to give the Princess an ever-widening picture of the industries of Britain.

QUEEN OF TO-MORROW

Though these visits are designed expressly as part of the education of the Princess, on each of them, so far, she has gone not alone but with Queen Mary, and the wise, experienced lead of her grandmother has been of incalculable value in many different ways. Officially, therefore, Princess Elizabeth has gone to the factories accompanying Queen Mary, since Her Majesty takes precedence of Her Royal Highness. Something of a stir was caused, accordingly, by the advance notice of one such visit, when an official with a slightly distorted sense of news-value issued a statement that "Princess Elizabeth, accompanied by Queen Mary" would be present. Queen Mary smiled at the sudden reversal of positions, but steps were taken to ensure that future announcements should read correctly, "Queen Mary, accompanied by Princess Elizabeth. . . ."

All these functions, including even the factory visit where the holiday atmosphere of a formal Royal occasion is deliberately discouraged, belong to the Princess's official life. They form part, and a large part, of her public duties. The people of Edinburgh, Cardiff, Belfast, Nottingham, Bedford, Sunderland, and Brighton, to name a few of the cities and towns which she has visited recently, know the Princess only as they see her driving to a hospital, to a civic centre, to a shipyard, or carrying out whatever ceremony she has been asked to perform. Londoners are more fortunate. It is true that so far she has only paid one official visit to the "square mile" of the City of London itself, in 1944, when on May 31, she went to the Mansion House, to be received by the Lord Mayor, Sir Frank Newsom-Smith, and to speak at the diamond jubilee meeting of the National Society for the Prevention of Cruelty to Children. But outside the City she is seen much more often, leaving Buckingham Palace in the morning, in the black Lanchester saloon from the Royal Mews which the King has put at her disposal till she has a car of her own, to pay her regular visit to her dentist, or to visit friends; and in the evening, at a theatre or occasionally at a restaurant with a party of friends. These last form a new side of the Princess's life, which must be considered separately in another chapter.

CHAPTER FIVE

The Princess Off-Duty

HOBBIES AND AMUSEMENTS

WHATEVER Princess Elizabeth may owe to Queen Victoria in her mental make-up, or to Queen Mary in the perfection of her physical colouring, it is from her great-grandfather, King Edward VII, that eager lover of life, that successful master of the difficult art of combining kingship with common humanity, that she inherits her love of two of her greatest outside amusements, the theatre and racing. Neither her grandfather, King George V, who used to complain that he could neither see nor hear from the Royal box where he had always to sit when he went to the play, nor her father ever showed much serious interest in the theatre. And for both King George V and his son the Royal racing stud has lacked that deep personal interest that King Edward maintained throughout his life—often, in his earlier days to the considerable annoyance of his mother, Queen Victoria—in all matters connected with racing. Judging by the indications she has given up to now, Princess Elizabeth seems likely to follow his example in both these spheres. Before she was old enough to go on a racecourse, the Princess used to follow keenly the progress of her father's horses, and when the King's much fancied colt Big Game failed to win the Derby at Newmarket in 1942, nowhere was there keener disappointment than in the Royal schoolroom, where Princess Elizabeth, then 16, heard the result from the wireless. As for the theatre, her early career as a successful producer of and player in pantomimes gave a clear pointer to where her interests would lie.

Since she began to go about on her own, Princess Elizabeth has amply confirmed both these early indications, and both the racing world and the world of the theatre are delighted to welcome her as their newest Royal patron.

Her first visit to a racecourse was appropriately to the Royal course at Ascot, where she went with her father to one of the wartime "austerity" meetings, that is to an ordinary race meeting run by the Jockey Club on the famous course which they leased for the purpose from the King, and not to a real Ascot "garden party" meeting with its fashion parade and its exclusive Royal enclosure. When Princess Elizabeth went to her first Ascot, on Whit Monday, May 21, 1945, the Royal lawn was open to the public. Men and women in service uniform, war-workers in tweed coats and grey flannels, and women in trousers, American soldiers of every rank from generals to G.I.s, men and women from the Dominion Forces, and from the armies of the allies, walked in the holiday crowds in front of the bow-fronted Royal box. But it was the racing, and not the crowds, which the Princess had come to see, and she very soon made it obvious that her attention was centred on the horses, following the races through binoculars, asking questions of her father, of the Duke of Norfolk, and of Captain Moore, manager of the King's thoroughbred stud. Then she walked down with the King through the crowds to see the horses saddled and the jockeys mounting. This was something she already knew a good deal about, for horse riding has been one of her keenest hobbies since her first lessons on the Shetland pony her grandfather

The Princess has always had a good seat and hands on horseback.

gave her for Christmas when she was four, and she not only rides well both side-saddle and astride, but is thoroughly competent to groom and saddle her own horse—as she frequently used to do.

To see the gaily-coloured jockeys perched high in their stirrups cantering purposefully down the course was a new thrill for her, and she remained in the front of the Royal box for the rest of the afternoon, watching every race until the time came for her to go home with her father to Windsor.

Next race the Princess saw was the Derby. It was a wartime Derby, though peace in Europe had already come, and instead of the real Epsom atmosphere that makes the great race one of the most outstanding experiences in the sporting world, she saw it in the tamer conditions of Newmarket, with no Tattenham Corner to trap the unwary, no costermongers on their barrows, no gipsies ready to foretell any amount of future events except the result of the race, none of the trimmings of Epsom. But still it was the test of the fastest and finest three-year-olds in the country, and the rapt expression on her face as she watched the hard fought finish, with the favourite Dante winning by two lengths from Midas told anyone who cared to look—and there were not a few who turned their glasses on the Royal box—that she was enjoying the experience to the full.

The secret of the Princess's skill as a rider to-day is that she learned very young. An early morning canter in Windsor Great Park.

These two visits made racing folk hope that the Princess was going to follow their sport. The next two made them sure she was. Crowds at Ascot in the paddock, watching the horses and jockeys preparing for the £1,000 Queen Mary Stakes, noticed a girl in khaki A.T.S. uniform in the saddling ring—and the news spread that the Princess was there. Actually, she had arrived on the course alone some time before, but scarcely anyone had noticed her in the Royal box. It was her first visit alone to the races, and this time, she was determined to see everything for herself. After one race, she was granted a privilege given to few women in the history of British racing, entry into the weighing room, the most jealously guarded place on a racecourse. She watched the jockeys being weighed in, highly amused to catch their looks of unbelieving surprise as they came, tired and sweating, their racing saddles under their arms, into the room to find a woman present. It was an experience neither they nor the Princess will ever forget.

Next time the Princess went racing, it was again to Ascot, this time with her father, to see the big double event of the Gold Cup and the Royal Hunt Cup run in the same programme. And this time, she clenched all arguments about the genuineness of her interest in racing by staying on alone when the King left after the second big race. She saw two more events, leaving just before the last race on the card, and then only because the police warned her that the crush of cars afterwards would be so bad they might have difficulty in clearing a way for her. She went to two more "austerity" Ascot meetings in the August Bank Holiday week-end, this time with both her mother and father.

After this, speculation began whether the Princess intended to set up a racing establishment of her own. For her to follow in the line of many of her Royal ancestors by buying a string of thoroughbreds for herself, or leasing them from the National stud, as her father has done, would be a tremendously popular move, which would endear her even more to the great racing public who have already taken her to their hearts as a "real young sport". But there is a racing tradition that children do not race against their parents, so the sight of a second version of the Royal colours on the course is a rather remote possibility.

The Princess, however this may be, shows no signs of letting her racing interest die down. In the autumn of 1945, she went alone to Newmarket, to watch the Royal hopes for the 1946 Classics at exercise on the Heath at the chilling hour of six a.m., afterwards attending the bloodstock sales, and then being on the course in time for the first race.

She went again to the "headquarters of racing" six months later, with the King to look over Palace House, formerly used as a racing box by Mr. Anthony de Rothschild, and again saw the Royal stud at early morning exercise gallops.

Latest proof of her keenness was when, after a visit to Sunderland, where she launched an oil tanker, she went by train on a difficult cross-country journey to Newmarket to attend the Guineas meeting. This journey meant using a full special train, in place of the single special coach attached to an ordinary express in which the Princess usually travels, since there were no direct trains from Sunderland to Newmarket.

It is, incidentally, another illustration of the affection in which the King holds his daughter that he gave her permission to use the Royal train itself for this journey.

These two visits to Newmarket races, coupled with an Easter Saturday visit to Hurst Park with the King, and her visit to the 1946 Oaks at Epsom with her parents, caused some superstitious racing folk to regard the Princess as a "luck-bringer". When she went to Newmarket in October 1944, they noted, the King's filly, Hypericum, won the Dewhurst Stakes. At Hurst Park, when she was with the King, Hypericum was beaten, but at Newmarket, with the Princess watching, again on her own, Hypericum carried off the One Thousand Guineas. When she went to her first Epsom, with the King and Queen, Hypericum was much fancied. But she could only finish fourth.

Princess Elizabeth herself has no such superstitions, and when her friends told her of the "luck" story, she just laughed. Her interest in racing is, indeed, centred on the horses themselves, their breeding and performance, and the skill and endurance of the jockeys, not on the financial results of a race. It is, however, freely stated in racing circles that the Princess usually has a bet on any big race she is watching, especially if there is a Royal entry with a chance: but her bets are by no means big ones.

Racing folk talking to the Princess have been surprised at the depth of her knowledge of bloodstock and breeding. When she went to the circus, too, she astonished the Mills brothers, who showed her round their stables, by recognising every breed of horse they had, with the single exception of a pair of Fresian blacks, a rare breed, not often seen in this country outside the circus. That is merely one more instance of her thoroughness and capacity for taking pains. When as a very young girl she began to be interested

Her thirteenth birthday: a morning ride at Windsor with her father and her sister

in the horses in the Royal Mews, she started to read all the books she could find pertaining to the subject, and to-day her knowledge in this respect as in others is wide and deep.

Though she is a first-class horsewoman herself, with an excellent seat and "easy" hands, the war robbed her of much opportunity for hunting and she has only once ridden to hounds, with her cousin, the Duke of Beaufort's pack, in the winter of 1943. Those who rode with her reported she had perfect manners in the field, took her fences boldly and well, kept up with hounds, but never attempted to overrun them. Most of her riding is done within the grounds of Windsor, Balmoral or Sandringham, often, when he is free, with the King, at other times with her sister Princess Margaret. On these occasions, both Princesses wear fawn jodhpurs, coats, and a silk scarf round the head.

Like all other horseriders, Princess Elizabeth has an occasional spill: but they are few and far between, and only once has she been prevented from fulfilling an engagement because of a riding mishap, when both her legs were badly bruised after she had been thrown from her horse against a tree at Balmoral in 1945.

Besides being a good rider, the Princess is a skilful and expert driver—an ability she put to good use when to save petrol during the war she and her sister did nearly all their journeys about Windsor in a pony cart. Twice, she won cups in the private driving class at the Royal Windsor Horse Show in successive years, first driving her dun-coloured Norwegian pony "Hans" in a smart black pony phaeton which had belonged to Queen Victoria, with Princess Margaret as her passenger, and next year, with her Blackfell pony "Gipsy" and a red and cream turn-out that was very attractive indeed. On both

these occasions, the King and Queen were spectators, and the King's keen eye was a guarantee, if one was needed, that the Princess won her events on merits and not by favouritism, the slightest suggestion of which would have called forth a severe Royal rebuff. In the second year, the Princesses, competing against each other in another class, were both unplaced.

In most informal, outdoor pictures of Princess Elizabeth, you will see a small, smooth-coated dog with her. It is either Crackers or Sue, the present day successors of Duke and Jane, her first pets, and, like them, pure-bred Welsh Corgi terriers, a faithful, intelligent, companionable breed which the Princess's choice did much to make popular.

Chin, a shaggy haired white dog of a much rarer breed, completes the Princess's "household" of pets. He is a Tibetan lion dog, which she has had since he was a tiny puppy.

Among her other athletic interests, swimming finds a high place. She learned when

Hans has a celebration drink : after Princess Elizabeth had won the private driving class at the Windsor Horse Show, 1944.

In her favourite riding kit, tweed coat, jodhpurs, and a silk scarf: Princess Elizabeth leaves Windsor Castle with her sister for a morning ride on the eve of her twentieth birthday.

she was very young, won the Children's Challenge Cup at the Bath Club when she was eleven, and gained their Life Saving Certificate. Four years later, she was the first candidate to gain the Royal Life Saving Society's artificial respiration award. At Buckingham Palace, not long before the war, the King had a private swimming pool built for her and Princess Margaret on the site of the old real tennis court. A German bomb destroyed it completely on November 1, 1940, and repairs are still a long way down the list of Royal priorities, but at Windsor there are plenty of opportunities for swimming.

Shooting is another of her outdoor interests. To the delight of the ghillies at Balmoral, it is the difficult and arduous art of deer-stalking that she most enjoys, with its long days on the hillside. She shot her first stag in September 1942, bringing down three in her first day's stalk, but she has still to attain the stalker's ambition of a Royal—a stag with twelve-point antlers.

First intimation the outside world had of Princess Elizabeth's interest in the theatre was an unheralded announcement that she had been with her sister and her own young lady-in-waiting, the Hon. Mrs. Vicary Gibbs, to the evening performance of Terence Rattigan's comedy *While the Sun Shines* on November 12, 1945. She had, of course, been to the theatre many times before,—she saw her first matinee, a fairy play, *Ever So Long Ago*, as a girl of nearly eight, with her mother at the Cambridge Theatre—but always with her parents. For her to go out alone in the evening was a new departure and next day, it was front-page news both in this country and in America, especially as there were four young Guards officers in her party in the fourth row of the stalls. That visit was the forerunner of many, and the catholicity of the Princess's taste in plays can be judged by the list of the first nine or ten she went to: Noel Coward's comedy *Private Lives: Duet for Two Hands*, a "thriller": *The Years Between*, a post-war problem play: Coward's musical show revue *Sigh No More*: Cicely Courtneidge's comedy *Under the Counter*: Ivor Novello's romantic *Perchance to Dream*: Wilde's *Lady Windermere's Fan*: *The Sleeping Princess Ballet* at Covent Garden: *The Hasty Heart*: and *The First Gentleman*, the play about her own ancestor George IV. And when she went to a matinee for King George's Fund for Actors, and the organisers asked her what she would prefer to see from the Old Vic repertoire, she surprised everyone by asking for Sophocles' tragedy *Oedipus* and Sheridan's comedy *The Critic*, both *pièces de théâtre* representing a connoisseur's choice.

When Princess Elizabeth goes officially to the theatre, tradition demands that she shall sit nowhere save in a box. But when she goes in private, and is free to sit where she likes, she emphatically refuses to use a box, preferring instead to sit in the stalls, usually the fourth or fifth row. In spite of the greater privacy which a box affords—for you have only to sit back in the intervals, and no one will know you are there—the Princess likes the stalls, where literally anyone may rub shoulders with her party, because she goes to the theatre to see the play, and, like many other theatre-lovers, she claims that from a box you cannot see the play as it is meant to be seen, since at best you have only a one-sided view of the stage.

Whether she goes officially to a special performance, or privately to an ordinary show, the Princess and her party always pay for their seats. So, incidentally, do the King

"*Princess Elizabeth and a Friend.*" *Corgi dogs are still her favourites, and this picture was taken at Glamis Castle in Coronation Year.*

With the grey stones of Windsor Castle in the background: Princess Elizabeth in her country tweeds takes Sue and Crackers for a morning walk.

and Queen, the only exception being the annual Royal Variety Performance, when Their Majesties are the invited guests of the Variety Artistes Benevolent Fund, which promotes the show.

For various reasons, the Princess does not like giving much advance notice of her private theatre visits, a habit which has more than once caused the managements of very successful shows to be hard put to it to find her the seats she wants. On one occasion at least, when the telephone call came through from Buckingham Palace to the manager's office in the morning, there was, literally, not a single seat unsold in the house. Some *might* be returned before evening, but that chance was too slender to be taken. So a harassed manager sat down to telephone everyone he knew personally who had seats for that evening, to ask them to put off their visit for the Princess to have their seats. . . . It took him an hour's hard telephoning, but the seats came back, and the Princess and her friends saw the show.

Another real "last-minute" visit was when the Princesses, who had already been to see Cicely Courtneidge in *Under the Counter* on their own persuaded the King and Queen to take them again, only a couple of hours before the show began. An equerry rang the theatre from the Palace rather anxiously, but this time luck was in, as two boxes were to be occupied by friends of the management. They came the following night.

Nothing has given greater pleasure to managers, actors and actresses, playwrights and playgoers alike than the Princess's keenness on the theatre, and she has won herself a place in the hearts of yet another section of the community by the absence of fuss or ceremony with which she goes to the play. One night, sitting in the stalls, a bride and bridegroom on honeymoon did not know the Princess was sitting next to them until the interval, and often the cast themselves do not know she is coming until the curtain has gone up. For her part, the Princess would be pleased if no one at all knew in advance of her theatre visits. She regards them, rightly, as part of her private life, and accordingly does not welcome unnecessary publicity, though of course, she is well aware

The King and his family study the programme : at the last of the King's Camps at Abergeldie, 1939.

A very informal picture : the Princess smoothes her father's wind-ruffled hair as they study maps before the Royal tour of Canada in 1939.

that the fact that she has been to see a play is a valuable advertisement for it, and therefore does not mind her presence being announced afterwards. But when she first began to go out in the evenings, Fleet Street was so keen on detailed descriptions of her dress and escorts that once, when she did not think anyone knew she was even in London, she arrived at the theatre to find three reporters in the stalls awaiting her!

After the play, the Princess likes to go on to supper and to dance, perhaps at a West-End restaurant, perhaps privately at the house of a friend. This, too, was big news at first and car loads of reporters laid in wait several times to follow the Princess to her destination. Regarding this as an unseemly and unnecessary intrusion into her private life, the Princess took steps to elude her Press pursuers by the simple but effective method of driving back to Buckingham Palace from the theatre, and leaving again a little later when the coast was clear. It was only one or two papers which adopted this course, and after a time they, too, decided that the Princess was entitled to have her wish for privacy, that rarest of treasures for those of Royal birth, respected.

Her lady-in-waiting, two of her young women friends, and four young men escorts usually make up the Royal theatre party, often including one of the several young married couples among the Princess's circle.

With a natural sense of rhythm, cultivated in a long series of lessons in every kind of dancing which began when she was a very small girl, it is not surprising that Princess Elizabeth is extremely fond of dancing. Fox-trots, tangos, rhumbas, old-fashioned waltzes, all come equally easily to her, and to watch her tread the intricate steps of a Highland eightsome reel to the skirling music of the bagpipes is to see dancing really enjoyed. With a complete mastery of the steps and patterns of the reel, the Princess will aid a less-expert partner confidently through his paces, keeping the whole set going, her face flushed and smiling, her movements rapid, graceful, exact and controlled, till she imbues every-one with her own spontaneous enthusiasm, and even the watchers by the side of the floor are beating time with her.

When she went to her first charity dance, the Princess asked for two reels to be included in the programme, and had the King's Piper from Buckingham Palace to play them, with the result that next day, fashionable dance teachers were invaded by scores of young men and women, all anxious to learn the reel, which by no means all the teachers were entirely familiar with themselves!

At private dances, particularly when it is a dance given for her at Buckingham Palace, or Windsor Castle, the Princess loves to lead a "Conga", the long line of dancers following her through the red-carpeted corridors and State apartments as the music wanes and waxes. The big ballroom on the first floor of the Palace, where in pre-war days debutantes made their first shy curtseys to the King and Queen, has not been used since it was shut up when war began. Instead, the white and gold Bow Saloon on the ground floor, which derives its name from the semi-circle of long French windows that open on to the Palace gardens, is used for dancing. The red carpets are taken up, the wooden floor polished, the band—one or other of the well-known dance bands is engaged for the evening—is stationed in an alcove at the side of the Grand Hall, there is a long buffet table with sandwiches, champagne and soft drinks, and such an atmosphere of jollity and gay enjoyment that it is not very difficult to imagine a smile on the face of young Queen Victoria, herself an eager dancer in her day, as she looks down on the scene from Winter-halter's painting hanging on one side of the arched entrance to the room, with his portrait of the Prince Consort on the other.

Sometimes, the Bow Saloon has been the scene of more impromptu dances, when the King and Queen and the Princesses, with a few friends, have had the carpets turned back, and danced to the music of gramophone records. And at one dance, Princess Elizabeth was enjoying herself so much that when the time came for the band to go home, she prevailed on her cousin, Captain the Hon. Andrew Elphinstone, who is an excellent pianist, to play for half an hour extra so that dancing might go on.

Apart from the Princess's own friends and acquaintances, quite a number of other folk have danced with her, including many Service officers, a sprinkling of Americans among them, who were invited to some of the wartime parties at Windsor Castle. One of the first partners she had outside her own circle was a sixteen year old drummer

Princess Elizabeth is a keen and accom

The Princesses watch the ballet : they sit side by side in the Royal box at the reopening night of Covent Garden Opera House to see the Sadler's Wells Company dance "The Sleeping Beauty".

boy who boldly asked her to dance a fox-trot on the evening of her sixteenth birthday, when, with the King and Queen, she paid a surprise visit to the Sergeants' Mess of the Grenadiers at Windsor Barracks, after being made Colonel of the Regiment that morning. Once a year, too, servants at the Palace have the chance of dancing with the Princess, when, again with her mother and father and sister, she attends the Christmas ball in the Servants' Hall. Old-time numbers, like the Valeta, the Palais Glide, and the St. Bernard Waltz are apt to appear on the programme at this function, but the Princess knows, and dances, them all.

Her favourite dance numbers vary with the taste and fashion of the moment, with one or two tunes with permanent places in her favour. These include "Night and Day", "Let's Fall in Love", and the modern version of "Sur Le Pont d'Avignon".

Noticeably absent from the list of the Princess's evening amusements is the cinema. She has not in fact yet been inside a London picture theatre, yet she has seen most modern films, and is well conversant with the current stars of Hollywood and the ᵇritish studios, a paradox explained by the fact that at Windsor Castle there is a fully-ᵉquipped projector and screen, where nearly every week there is a private showing ᵗʰᵉ latest films often before their public release, for the Royal family and their guests, of modern version of the "Command Performances" with which Queen Victoria entertain her Court when she was young. Talking to young naval officers at a cruiser's wardroom, she evinced a preference for "Westerns", especially ʳⁱⁿg Mr. Gary Cooper, and a decided liking for Mr. David Niven's acting ʸ Ahead".

One of her first supper parties in a smart West End restaurant after the play.

The Princess is interested, too, in amateur cine-photography. She has a camera of her own, spools from which, recording family activities of the King and Queen and Princess Margaret, would command their own price in Hollywood. But they, of course, are for private exhibition only. Probably the most historic film the Princess has taken is the one which she "shot" on VJ Day from the crimson-hung balcony of Buckingham Palace. Unguessed at by the massed crowds below chanting "We want the King, We want the King . . ." the Princess stood a little concealed in the long windows, filming the scene around the Victoria Memorial and along the Mall. It is the first film of a great national celebration ever to be taken by a member of the Royal family from the Palace itself, and one day, perhaps, the Princess may permit this one, at least, to be shown.

Of more serious amusements, music ranks easily first with the Princess. She plays the piano with real skill and a natural talent that she has encouraged by years of constant study and practice. At Buckingham Palace, the Princess has two grand pianos, one in her own apartments, the other down in the State rooms, on which she plays, sometimes alone, sometimes duets with her sister or with the Queen. There is a grand for her use at Windsor as well. Visitors at the Palace or the Castle for the first time often stop in the corridors, enchanted by the music, wondering who is playing. . . . The Princess sings, too, in a pleasant, well-modulated, true voice of moderate volume and pleasing tone, delighting most in old English and Scottish songs, which she learned at her mother's knee. Recently, she has arranged a series of madrigal parties at the Palace, at which a number of her friends with good voices join in the singing of old traditional airs like "Greensleeves," "Blow, Blow Thou Winter Wind," and other Shakespearian songs, with Dr. Harris, the organist from St. George's Chapel Windsor, conducting. Bach, Chopin, Beethoven, all the great masters of the past, Barthok, Ravel, Delius, and the leading modernists, all are the Princess's familiars. It is from her mother, who played the piano and the harp as a small girl, that she inherits her love of music, and it was the Queen who first instilled into her small head, then covered with fair curls, the beginnings of musical knowledge and appreciation. To-day, there is probably nothing that gives the Queen truer pleasure than to sit for a while, with the cares of majesty put aside, and listen to her daughter playing, the notes cascading in the still Palace air, poising, building into intricate patterns, resolving into simple themes and cadences under the Princess's deft, strong fingers. . . . Sometimes, when she is free from her lessons, Princess Margaret joins her, and the Royal sisters play duets on two pianos.

It was, therefore, as an expression of her genuine interest in and love of things musical that Princess Elizabeth accepted as her first fully fledged public post that of President of the Royal College of Music in October 1943. To show that it was no sinecure appointment which she had taken up, but one in which she meant to take a practical interest, she went to the Jubilee Concert of the College shortly after her appointment, to present the prizes and certificates to winning students, while the Queen watched from the centre of the balcony. This was her first experience of distributing prizes, and it was also the first time she had carried out a public engagement under the eyes of her mother, so it was no wonder that at first, the Princess, standing a little shyly in her lonely eminence on the red-covered dais, was considerably more nervous than any of the young men and women students who filed past her. But her nervousness lasted for only a very short while, and after half a dozen or so had shaken hands with her and taken their prizes, she found herself quite at ease. Since then, the Royal President has continued to take an active interest in all the affairs of the College.

Another illustration of her love of music lies in her acceptance of an honorary degree from the University of London. Royalty, in common with distinguished figures in many different fields of human activity, sometimes receive academic honours qualifying them as Doctors of subjects about which they know but little. D.Ll.'s (Hon.) to whom the law is a closed book, and D.Litt.'s (Hon.) who have read neither widely or deeply, are not unknown. In this, as in so many other matters, Princess Elizabeth has taken her own independent line. Her knowledge of law, certainly of constitutional law, is by no means small, and her knowledge of English and French literature is, as we have seen, extensive. But it was the cap and light blue gown of a Bachelor of Music which she accepted from her great-uncle, the Earl of Athlone, Chancellor of the University, at the ceremony in the Senate House, and though she had passed no examination for her honorary degree, she could legitimately feel that she was sailing under no false colours in accepting it, for, had she been permitted by circumstances to study at a University, music would undoubtedly have been one of her chief and favourite subjects.

CHAPTER SIX

The Fairy Tale of Windsor

WHEN "PRINCE CHARMING" WAS A REAL PRINCESS

WHEN Shakespeare wrote, sighing for the impossible, "a kingdom for a stage, princes to act, and monarchs to behold the swelling scene," it was of the high drama of Agincourt he was thinking. Four centuries later, at Windsor Castle, the dramatist's dream of the unattainable came to reality, though it was no high drama, but a Christmas pantomime, which brought the heiress of England and her sister on to the stage, and set the sovereign of England and his consort laughing in the stalls.

For four years running, from 1941 to 1944, Princess Elizabeth and Princess Margaret helped to write, stage and produce a pantomime each Christmas, playing the leading parts themselves, and the story of these, surely the most astonishing pantomimes that have ever been staged, is itself rather like a fairy tale, though a fairy tale in reverse, with the real Princess revelling in the part of Principal Boy, instead of the young actress dreaming of the delightful life she would lead if she were a real and not a stage Princess. It began with the erection of a stage at the Castle for the use of various artistes whom the King summoned to Windsor to provide entertainment and relaxation for his family and for the many Court officials, clerks and servants evacuated there from London, and unable to get to theatres or cinemas. Into Princess Elizabeth's fertile mind, as she talked to the famous players whom she met after their performances, came the idea of giving an entertainment herself with Princess Margaret and some of their friends, the kind of idea that many people get after watching a good show—and then do nothing about it. But with the Princess it was different. She is a firm believer in putting thought into action and within a few days, when she had secured her father's permission, plans were being discussed, Castle officials consulted, rehearsals arranged. That first show in 1940 was a simple nativity play in which the two Princesses sang.

It was such a success that Princess Elizabeth decided on a more ambitious scheme for the next year, and determined to have a pantomime of her own.

By chance, at the Royal School in the Windsor Home Park, where the children of workers on the Royal estates are educated, was the very man to help, the headmaster, Mr. Hubert Tannar, whose great hobby was amateur theatricals. With his aid, a script was written, a cast chosen, and *Cinderella*, the first of the Royal pantomimes, was under way. Princess Elizabeth put her energies whole-heartedly into the job as she has the habit of doing with everything she tackles, and "script conferences", rehearsals, dance and song "try-outs" began to occupy more and more of the out-of-study hours of both Princesses, for Princess Margaret, who has both shrewd powers of observation and a keen wit of her own, took her full share in all these activities, particularly in the script writing. Cinderella was a well-enough worn theme, but, in the true tradition of pantomime, the Princesses decided that anything and everything might be dragged into

The Royal sisters dressed for a ballroom scene in their pantomime. Each Princess is wearing real pearls.

the story, provided it made for laughter. Family jokes with hidden allusions, references to the latest war developments, sly friendly quips about members of the Household, all went into the "book", which no one outside the cast was allowed to know anything about in advance. And whenever anyone who might be considered to know about theatrical matters arrived at the Castle, Princess Elizabeth made a point of asking their advice on some of her problems. Arthur Askey, George Formby, and Miss Florence Desmond were some of the Princess's "consultants" in this respect.

Like other wartime producers, the Princess and her companions had to face the twin problems of scenery and dresses. Members of the Castle staff, delighted to help, set to and stitched clothes and costumes from all sorts of scrap material, while the superintendent of the Castle, Mr. Stanley Williams, and his staff took on the task of making and painting backcloths, scenery, and various property effects. Most of the casting problems were comparatively easy. Princess Elizabeth would be Prince Charming, Princess Margaret, Cinderella, the schoolmaster enthusiast, the senior comedian, while other parts could go to the Princess's friends, with the Royal School children to provide the chorus. But there remained the problem of a young comedian to play opposite the Princesses, and here the story of the Royal pantomimes takes on a more fairy-tale quality than ever, for it was a young office-boy in the Supply Department of the Castle who was selected by the Princess for this part. Cyril Woods, then aged fifteen, had been such a success in the first Christmas concert, that he was the obvious choice, and so well did he acquit himself that in each of the three succeeding pantomimes, he remained the star comedian, playing Widow Twankey to Princess Elizabeth's Aladdin, and Old Mother Hubbard to her Lady Christina. Details of the first pantomimes were kept semi-secret, but later, when the King allowed reports to appear mentioning Cyril Woods, and telling the story of the Princess and the office boy, theatrical and film agents began to be interested in him. Unmoved by all this publicity and fuss, the level-headed young man, with a natural gift for mimicry that many professionals would envy, went back each year to his office work as a junior, addressing quite minor members of the staff as "Sir" the day after he had been acting and joking with the two Princesses. It was a situation in which Barrie —Princess Margaret's long-established favourite author—would have taken delight, a situation which could occur nowhere else in the world save at the Court of the King of England.

To-day, when the last of the pantomimes has been played, Woods is still at work in an office as a junior, in the Accountants Department at Buckingham Palace. Sometimes as he checks bills and goes about his daily routine task, he must think back to those amazing days when the King's two daughters stood back to give him the centre of the stage . . .

For Princess Elizabeth and Princess Margaret, each of the pantomimes was a personal triumph. The Royal sisters sing and dance together extremely well; indeed, singing duets to the King and Queen is a favourite enjoyment of theirs, but there is a considerable difference between that and appearing on a stage, and it was a fully equipped, large stage, with footlights, spotlights, curtains, changing scenery and other effects on which the Princesses played their parts to an audience including besides the King and Queen and other members of their family, scores of strangers, and, at one performance each year, detachments of Guardsmen from Windsor Barracks who came by special invitation from Princess Elizabeth. It was not, therefore, the easiest of audiences, but the Princesses, especially Princess Margaret, played with a lack of self-consciousness that was delightful to watch, throwing themselves completely in their parts. To hear them in the last of their pantomimes, *Old Mother Red Riding Boots*, a happy mixture of half a dozen traditional pantomime stories, sing the old French nursery rhyme, "Sur le Pont d'Avignon" in "The Glade of the Crystal Stream" was an unforgettable experience. First they sang it in the original manner as a nursery rhyme, then in modern "swing" time, in which guise "Sur le Pont" is one of Princess Elizabeth's favourite dance tunes. They sang, in that same pantomime, "Come into the Garden, Maud", and here too, all was not quite as the original composer intended, for "Lady Christina Sherwood" (Princess Elizabeth) and "The Hon. Lucy Fairfax" (Princess Margaret) sang Tennyson's love poem in broad Cockney accents which would have made the refined Poet Laureate squirm, but which the 1944 audience enjoyed to the full—none more than the King, who laughed till the tears really did start in his eyes.

At all the pantomimes, the King was one of the most enthusiastic onlookers, attending the dress rehearsals and each of the two or three performances to which they were limited.

The simple, good-natured, straightforward humour made a direct appeal to him, and from nowhere in the crowded "house" came louder laughs than from the front row where the King and Queen sat side by side. Playing Aladdin, Princess Elizabeth, who shares with her father a respect for the traditional and proper way of doing things, made her entrance by popping out of a laundry basket, as Aladdins have been wont to do for many a decade: and when, a little later, "Aladdin" remarked to "his" friends, "I don't know *what* they've been doing up at the Castle lately, they have so much washing every week", the King thoroughly enjoyed the joke, all the more because at that time, soap and labour shortages made the Castle laundry much less than in peace time. Another home allusion which brought gusts of laughter from the King and Queen came in the same show, when Aladdin and Princess Roxana (Princess Margaret) discussed the "Coronation paintings" of the "Emperor and Empress" by "Sir Kerald Jelly" who, explained Princess Roxana to Aladdin, was finding great difficulty in getting the likenesses of his sitters exactly as he wanted—a reference to the painstaking care with which Sir Gerald Kelly, R.A., was even then, in 1943, completing his State paintings of the Coronation scene in May 1937.

Popular tunes of the moment are always sung at Christmas pantomimes: and Princess Elizabeth followed ritual in this as well, sometimes altering the words to more appropriate phrasing. "In my Arms", "It's Foolish, but it's Fun", "Swinging on a Star", "Red, White and Blue Christmas" and other numbers of a similiar kind figured in the programmes.

Ballet dancing has been an interest of Princess Elizabeth's since her very early years, when she had her first dancing lessons at 145, Piccadilly, and pas-de-deux by her and her sister were a feature of each of the shows. Both Princesses dance elegantly and gracefully, Princess Elizabeth particularly being an excellent tap dancer. For their last pantomime, the Princesses decided on a more ambitious dance programme than before. This time, they had a whole corps de ballet, eleven in number, trained and produced by Madame Vacani, the Princesses' own instructress, in a delightful ballet of the seaside in the 'nineties, with Princess Elizabeth at her most charming in a becoming long-skirted Victorian dress of pink, and a small brimmed straw hat, dancing a waltz with a "beau" in gay blazer and white flannels. Princess Margaret appeared as a schoolgirl of the period, and the other dancers were Misses Louise Cockcraft, Anne Crichton, Mary Morshead, Phoebe Morshead, Joan Parker, Dawn Simpson, Anne Verney, Carola Verney, and Karla Whetherall.

For this pantomime, *Old Mother Red Riding Boots*, Princess Elizabeth called in other professional advice as well. Mr. Vincent Korda and Mr. F. Bellan made scenery and effects for the show in a film studio, which resulted in a pleasant Christmas surprise for the Princesses, when Mr. Korda took over to Windsor a complete working model of their stage set, and asked them to accept it as a souvenir. She ordered costumes from a famous theatrical firm, wigs from another, and persuaded Mr. R. H. Wood, the B.B.C. sound engineer who supervises the King's broadcasts, to arrange for sound reproduction.

Historians of the future may find themselves baffled when they come upon evidence of another delightful touch inspired by the Princess for this occasion. All the pantomimes took place in the famous Waterloo Chamber of Windsor Castle, a lofty, well-proportioned room, within whose walls successive sovereigns have received each year, on June 18, anniversary of the battle, the silken Union Jack which forms the rent paid by the Iron Duke and his successors for the Wellington estates of Strathsfieldspey, and where, on

THE FAIRY TALE OF WINDSOR

Waterloo Night it has been the custom to hold a state banquet in commemoration of the victory, with a hundred and fifty guests sitting at one huge mahogany table.

This room was built early in the nineteenth century on what had been an open court-yard, and the lofty walls of the surrounding buildings made a lantern light necessary, and ruled out windows. Its windowless walls are panelled with portraits of famous men of Napoleonic days, leaders of the Allied Powers who were victorious in 1814. King George III and King George IV, both in Garter robes, the first Duke of Wellington, Field Marshal von Blucher, the Emperor Alexander I of Russia, the Emperor Francis I of Austria, and King Frederick William III of Prussia, Prince Metternich, with generals, Cabinet ministers and plenipotentiaries, painted by Sir Thomas Lawrence, the President

*"Smile, please, and quite still!" The seaside photographer arranges his group:
an incident in the pantomime ballet.*

of the Royal Academy, by order of the Prince Regent, look down from the high walls. To preserve these paintings from possible bomb damage, they were removed with other Royal art treasures at the beginning of the war to a place of safety, and the high walls were left bare, with only the empty gilt frames to mark the vacant places, with the name of each portrait and its painter inscribed underneath.

Looking at these ugly empty spaces one day as she was making preliminary arrangements for the *Old Mother Red Riding Boots* pantomime, Princess Elizabeth had an idea. Why should they not be filled, temporarily at any rate, with paintings appropriate to the pantomime?

A few weeks later, from the ornate frames that had housed the effigies of the men who beat Napoleon, a new and startling series of faces looked out, Aladdin rubbing his magic

WATERLOO CHAMBER
WINDSOR CASTLE

⚬

A Christmas Pantomime

"Old Mother
Red Riding Boots"

December 21st, 22nd and 23rd, 1944

DEVISED BY

Princess Elizabeth, Princess Margaret
and Hubert Tannar

THE "SALON ORCHESTRA" OF
THE ROYAL HORSE GUARDS (THE BLUE

(By permission of Col. R. E. S. Gooch)

Under the Direction of Capt. A. J. Thornburrow

Stage Manager : Stanley A. Williams

Price 1/-

Old

Lady Chr
The Hono
Mother H
Sammy Su
Broker's M
Sir Marmad
Dona Salam
Fairy . . . . .
Betty Blosso

Fairflint (the

BETTY ASHTON—
DORIS MARSHAL

RONALD ALDRIDG
DENNIS NUTLEY

PRINCESS ELIZAB
ANNE CRICHTON, M
DAWN SIMPSON, AN

S
VIN
Sound R
COS

COSTUMES—
Danc
Wall Decorations de
assisted by the

ther Red Riding Boots

CHARACTERS

…erwood	PRINCESS ELIZABETH
…ucinda Fairfax	PRINCESS MARGARET
	CYRIL WOODS
	HUBERT TANNAR
	FREDERICK SMITH
…ntmorency	ANNE CRICHTON
…l Castellianos	MARY MORSHEAD
	DORIS MARSHALL
	VIOLET HELPS
	DAVID PRESCOTT
	CYRIL STURGES

CHORUS

…BUCKLAND, SHEILA COLLINGS, VIOLET HELPS,
…PEARCE, PHYLLIS PRATLEY, SYLVIA PULLIN,
 SYBIL STURGES

…ELLIOTT, JUNIOR FINLAYSON, LEONARD HELPS,
…T PEARCE, DENNIS QUADLING, KENNETH
…RDSON, DONALD SIDDLE

BALLET

…RINCESS MARGARET, LOUISE COCKCRAFT,
…RSHEAD, PHOEBE MORSHEAD, JOAN PARKER,
…TEY, CAROLA VERNEY, KARLA WHETHERALL

…y designed and made by
…KORDA and F. BELLAN
…n by R. H. WOOD of B.B.C.
…by L. and H. NATHAN
…y NATHANWIGS
… Ballet by MISS W. FELLOWES,
…ellet by MISS VACANI
…d painted by CLAUDE WHATHAM
…f the Wycombe Technical Institute

ACT I
Outside Ye Olde Wishinge Welle Inn

OPENING CHORUS	..	"Here We Are Again"
CHORUS	..	
SONG AND DANCE (*Lucinda*)	..	"Sing a Song of To-morrow To-day"
DUET AND DANCE	..	"It's Foolish, but it's Fun"
CHORUS (*Christina, Lucinda and Chorus*)	..	"Swinging on a Star"
FINALE, ACT I (*Christina, Lucinda and Chorus*)	..	"The Yeomen of England"

INTERLUDE
BALLET
Place : AT THE SEASIDE
Time : THE 1890's
Characters :

THE THREE BELLES	THE NURSE
THE THREE BEAUX	THE SAILOR
THE LITTLE GIRL	THE PHOTOGRAPHER
THE LITTLE BOY	

ACT II
The Glade of the Crystal Stream

SCENA (*The Tinies*)	..	"Easter Bunnies"
DUET AND DANCE (*Christina and Monty*)	..	"Shepherdess and Beau Brocade"
DUET (*Christina and Lucinda*)	..	"Sur le Pont d'Avignon"
FINALE, ACT II	..	"Sing a Song of To-morrow To-day"

ACT III—Scene 1
On the Road to Ascot

SONG (*Sammy*)	..	"My Motter"

ACT III—Scene 2

SONG (*Mother Hubbard and Chorus*)		"The Quack Quack Song"
TRIO (*Christina, Lucinda and Mother Hubbard*)	..	"Get your Guitar"

GRAND FINALE

FINALE	..	"Red, White and Blue Christmas"

"GOD SAVE THE KING"

As a Victorian belle in becoming dress, she inspects the "catch" of Princess Margaret and her friend in the pantomime ballet. Note the correct detail of all the dresses.

lamp, Mother Goose, her head apprehensively cocked, Cinderella in her glass slippers, and other familiar figures from the fairy land of make-believe. They had been painted by Mr. Claude Whatham assisted by students from the Wycombe Technical Institute, in gay colours with a touch of fantasy that was exactly right. The Princess's idea was a great success. The pantomime figures on the walls added the needed background that had been missing before—though no one else had noticed it—to complete the transformation of the state room into a theatre. When the opening show of the pantomime came, everyone was loud in praise of the new scheme of decorations, and all was well.

That was in December 1944. Six months later, with the war in Europe over, when the Royal paintings began to return to Windsor Castle from their safe hiding place, among them Lawrence's studies of George III, George IV, their brother monarchs and their generals, the question came, what was to be done with the pantomime paintings in their frames. The King ruled that they should stay where they were. Perhaps his sense of humour was aroused at the thought of how shocked the proud Prussian feelings of Frederick William III would be on finding himself sharing a frame with Aladdin: and to-day, unguessed at by sightseers visiting the Castle, behind the solemn, formal paintings of the men who conquered at Waterloo and rewrote the history of Europe, are hidden the happy smiling figures of childhood's dreams. . . .

Some ungenerous-minded people seemed to find it contrary to their peculiar conceptions of what is proper and fitting for a King's daughter that Princess Elizabeth and her sister should be allowed to appear on the stage, even in the setting of their own home. Such false ideas of the necessity for cottonwool wrapping round the whole lives of Royalty have never found favour with the King and Queen. If Princess Elizabeth enjoyed the

106

With the ballet in her last pantomime. Princess Elizabeth as a Victorian belle of the 'nineties.

harmless amusement, they saw, of course, no reason to interfere; instead, they encouraged her and Princess Margaret in every way, believing that the active work of creating and producing the shows, as well as the many contacts they brought about could be of nothing but benefit to their daughters.

The King became, as any father would, justly proud of his daughters' success: for it emphatically was a success that the Princesses scored each year. They danced and sang and mimed with such zest, such good stage sense, such excellence of rhythm and tune and time that their show, transferred to the West End as a children's performance, would easily have held its own. Each performance was singularly free from the wrong entries, the forgotten lines, the missed cues that usually mar amateur efforts of the kind. Princess Elizabeth saw to that. Setting herself the highest of standards, tireless in practice and re-hearsal, she asked for—and obtained—equal enthusiasm from the rest of the cast, and no one watching the rehearsals could be left in doubt for long of her observant eye and powers of control. On the stage or off, Princess Elizabeth seemed to see everything that was going on. Was there a false step by one of the chorus, a fluffed line by a minor character, a piece of scenery wrongly placed, she was the first to notice and have it put right. That characteristic painstaking attention to detail by the Princess was one of the two secrets of the pantomime's success. The other was that everyone in the show, from the principal players to the scene shifters—and certainly the orchestra of the Royal Horse Guards who provided the music—thoroughly enjoyed being in it. Each year, after the last performance, the Princess gave a Christmas tea party to the whole cast, making a little speech of thanks to them for their co-operation and help. And there was equal, if unexpressed, gratitude to her on the part of them all for giving them the oppor-tunity for so much fun.

PROGRAMME

OF

Christmas Pantomime

ALADDIN

IN THE

WATERLOO CHAMBER
WINDSOR CASTLE

DECEMBER 16th, 17th and 18th, 1943

PRICE 1s.

It is probably from Queen Victoria, who was in her younger days, much addicted to the theatre, frequently "commanding" famous actors and actresses to appear before her at Windsor, that the Princesses inherit their love of the stage. But the Royal family tradition of acting goes back a long way further than that. The three children of Charles I—the brothers, who became Charles II and James II, and the daughter, Princess Henrietta Maria—often acted in plays at the Palace of Whitehall to an audience of their father's courtiers and Ministers, and, later, King George III used to take part with other members of the Royal family in plays and presentations at Leicester House, coached by the famous actor Quin, and afterwards by Mrs. Siddons.

After *Old Mother Red Riding Boots*, however, there were to be no more Royal pantomimes. Princess Elizabeth was nearly nineteen when she made her appearance as "Lady Christina Sherwood" in that pantomime, and Princess Margaret, too, appeared as a girl, the "Hon. Lucinda Fairfax", with no principal boy in the cast. As pantomimes without principal boys are both difficult to devise and distinctly out of tradition, Princess Elizabeth decided, albeit with considerable reluctance, that her days as a pantomime star must come to an end—and the "Royal Company" dissolved. In any case, with the growing pressure of public duties, there would be little time in the future for the long hours of preparation, the talks and conferences, the script writing, the rehearsals, the hard work of production, which brought her as much enjoyment as the finished performances themselves. For the Princess, it was the end of an experience of great happiness and fun, one which she will remember all the days of her life.

CHAPTER SEVEN

Princess in Khaki

HALF a dozen lines of an official announcement issued from Buckingham Palace just over a month before her nineteenth birthday revealed the surprising news that Princess Elizabeth had joined the Auxiliary Territorial Service, and was taking a driving course.

The news was surprising because, twelve months before, the nation had been given clearly to understand that for the Princess, entry into any of the three women's services, or any other form of normal war service, was out of the question, since the claims of her training as heiress to the throne must come first. In the year that had passed, the public, almost without exception, had come to accept this decision as wise and right. Now, apparently, there was a complete reversal of Royal policy. The terms of the Palace announcement did nothing to clear up the mystery. It ran simply in these words:—"The King has granted to Her Royal Highness the Princess Elizabeth a commission with the honorary rank of second subaltern in the Auxiliary Territorial Service. Her Royal Highness is at present undergoing a course at a driving training centre in the south of England." The pith of the matter was in a semi-official adjunct to the announcement, which stated that this step had been taken "at the Princess's own request."

Behind those few words lies a revealing story of the strength of Princess Elizabeth's character, a story of how a Royal girl's determination caused a decision, made with Cabinet approval, to be reversed.

One by one, as war went on, she had seen her girl friends following their fathers and brothers—and in some cases their mothers as well—into the Services, joining one or other of the three women's services. When they came on leave, she heard from them the stories of new interests, new adventures, new companionships that homecoming warriors have told ever since the world was young, adventures and interests that she herself could never share, because, as she well knew, it had been decided that the necessity for her training for public life and future queenship to go on without interruption outweighed all other considerations, was of greater importance than any other form of service to the nation which she could possibly undertake.

As a subject of His Majesty, even though she happened to be the King's elder daughter, the Princess came under the provisions of the National Service Act, and had, indeed, registered for service as a junior at the age of sixteen. But hers was obviously a special case, requiring the personal consideration and attention of the Minister of Labour and National Service, Mr. Ernest Bevin, himself, and, doubtless, that of his colleagues in Mr. Churchill's Cabinet. After long and careful consideration, with the sanction of the King, and, therefore, the implicit approval of the War Cabinet, an official statement was issued from Buckingham Palace, on the eve of the Princess's eighteenth birthday, setting forth the position, and explaining why it had been decided that she should neither join one of the women's services, nor work at a munitions factory, as nearly all other girls of eighteen were doing. Only people with the most prejudiced of minds could find fault with this

Honorary Second Subaltern: a studio portrait of the Princess in khaki

eminently reasonable ruling, which gained general approval throughout the country and the Empire.

But there was one person at least who did not take a good view of it at all; and that was Princess Elizabeth. She could not, of course, make her dissentient voice heard in public: but in private, a good deal must have been going on behind the scenes in the way of argument and persuasion, until, a year later, the Princess scored a real personal triumph by gaining from her father a commission in the A.T.S. Though but few people realised it at the time, the announcement of her appointment was a direct pointer to a very important feature in the make-up of the heiress to the throne, her decided, determined character, and her no small measure of ability to get her own way in the face of strong opposition. It showed, too, that the Princess has the same gift of Royal intuition as her father, that instinctive understanding of what is the right thing to do, sometimes even against official advice, that is one of the corner stones of the British monarchy's strength.

Her decision was widely popular, and the way in which she carried it out more popular still, for the King, giving his consent to the appointment, had stipulated that his daughter should be treated in exactly the same way as any other officer trainee at the training centre. She was to receive no special privileges because of her personal rank, any more than the King himself did when he served in the Royal Navy and the Royal Air Force. From the first day she arrived at the private house, lying just off the main road into Camberley, which was the headquarters of No. 1 Mechanical Transport Training Centre of the A.T.S., Princess Elizabeth herself insisted that these orders should be strictly interpreted, and soon made it clear that she would dislike any attempt to make things easier for her because she was of Royal birth. In this connection, one point had to be given special consideration. Besides the normal wartime security silence, it was necessary to take extra precautions to guard the Princess's privacy, if gaping crowds were to be avoided. Sightseers following her every movement as she worked, or driving behind her when she was out under instruction, would have completely defeated the whole plan for her training, so, a few days before she was due to join the course, the commandant of the centre, a woman of wide experience, called all her officers together, told them of the honour that had been done their centre, and pointed out the imperative need for secrecy about the Princess's coming among them. The officers told the other ranks that evening, not even putting them on their honour, but leaving it to their own good sense and judgment not to talk. These steps resulted in a proof that a thousand girls *can* keep a secret, for even in the neighbouring town of Camberley a mile or so away, no one knew or even suspected the Princess was in camp until after the official announcement.

Not only the thousand lucky ones whose period at No. 1 Training Centre coincided with the Princess's stay, but girls in the A.T.S. all over the country were naturally delighted when they heard that the King's daughter had chosen their service in preference to the other two. The A.T.S. was, dare it be suggested, the third, rather than the first, choice of most fashionable young women on enrolling. The Princess had received her pre-entry training as a Sea Ranger, which clearly marked her out as a future candidate for the W.R.N.S., and she certainly enjoyed that advantage which was almost a *sine qua non* for the women's branch of the senior service, a father who was a naval officer. Perhaps the influence of her aunt, the Princess Royal, who devoted her energies so whole-heartedly throughout the war to the work of the A.T.S., of which she is Controller Commandant, is not without its bearing in this connection, or perhaps the Princess, wishing to make entirely new contacts, preferred to seek new experience in a service whose ways and methods were completely novel to her.

Whatever was the cause, it was the A.T.S. which the Princess chose, to the high and undisguised delight of all the other girls in khaki throughout the length and breadth of the land, and it is on record that the angle of tilt of the A.T.S. noses was noticeably higher in the week or two following the announcement of her choice.

Once she had made her decision, the Princess carried it through purposefully and thoroughly. Up till then, it is doubtful whether the hands of the daughter of a reigning sovereign had ever been soiled with car oil and gear grease, but when the practical side of the instruction course involved dismantling and reassembling engines, re-timing valves, changing wheels on heavy lorries, and the rest of the more unpleasant tasks that are usually relegated to chauffeurs or garage mechanics, the Princess did not falter, or shirk at the thought of grimy hands. On the contrary, she was intensely proud of the signs of mechanical toil on her hands, which she showed to her friends with great glee. She set to with a will, and was immensely pleased when, after the first day or two of constraint had passed, the other girls —who, incidentally, called her at her own request simply "Princess" and not "Your Royal Highness", if they were of equal or higher rank, and plain "Ma'am" as they did any other officer in the case of lower ranks—accepted and treated her as one of themselves. It was a test, and a test of a very special kind, for the Princess. She passed that exceptionally difficult test in human relationships with as full, if not fuller, marks as she did the driving and theory tests that ended her course.

The Princess enjoyed everything about her new life, and quickly made friends with a number of her fellow pupils. She took the altered conditions of life in her stride, settling down on the easiest of terms with her senior officers, her equals, and her subordinates alike. But if the Princess could take it all calmly, not all the rest of the A.T.S. could follow her example, as instance the case of one veteran girl-driver, herself an ex-pupil of No. 1 M.T. Centre, who had to drive a very senior A.T.S. officer down on a visit of inspection to see how the Royal pupil was progressing.

Just as she was backing her car into position after dropping her passenger, the A.T.S. driver saw Princess Elizabeth run down the steps of the officers' mess and get into the driving seat of an Army car, exactly similar to the one she was driving. It was the first time the A.T.S. girl had ever seen the Princess, and that, coupled with the thought that the King's daughter was doing the same job as she was, proved too much for her. Forgetting in her curiosity and excitement one of the chief rules she had learned at the Centre, she took her eyes off where she was going to look at the Princess. Her car crashed into a marking post, knocking it sideways. Princess Elizabeth, who misses very little of what goes on around her, saw the incident and smiled. By good fortune for the driver, no one else had seen what happened, and later she drove off with her officer-passenger without the reprimand she knew she had earned. But the leaning post was left leaning for some days, as an example to other drivers to attend to the job in hand no matter who might be passing.

The Princess's working hours were the same as for the rest of the "cadre", from 10 a.m. to 5 p.m. Each day ended with a routine cleaning of the vehicle she had been using, a check up on the oil, battery and radiator levels, and an engine test for smooth running.

At the start of an engine-maintenance lesson: the Princess, in her khaki working overalls, smiles happily by the open bonnet of her instruction car. In half an hour, her hands will not be so clean!

Photograph: Crown Copyright Reserved

PRINCESS IN KHAKI

In overalls, Princess Elizabeth takes a spell during an A.T.S. vehicle maintenance class.

When she began instruction, she was a complete novice, her driving experience confined entirely to being a passenger in the Royal limousines and an occasional ride in her father's private car. Some of her fellow students were novices, too, but the majority were already-qualified drivers, taking an N.C.O.'s refresher course. The Princess's two companions in her "syndicate" were sergeants, one with a husband fighting in the artillery in Italy.

The Army does not believe that the easiest way is always the best, and the first vehicle Princess Elizabeth had to handle was a fifteen hundredweight Army truck on blocks. When she had mastered the controls sufficiently, she went out on the roads, in trucks, six-cylinder motor ambulances, and staff cars, to gain experience of all types, driving at night in the appalling black-out conditions, as well as on the traffic-thronged roads by day. Besides all this she had to learn the whole theory of the "Otto cycle", the working of differentials and universal joints, gear-boxes and clutches, all the arcana of the internal combustion engine and its accessories which most motorists are well content to leave as mysteries as long as the car continues to go. She studied map reading, the highway code, and similar subjects. When the instructress would give the class a map reference to locate, it was open to any girl to put her hand up first—but only rarely was the Princess beaten. She has a naturally quick intelligence, which she was using to such good purpose

H

that the Commandant declared "All of us here have found the Princess extremely quick to learn. When she came, she had never driven a car of any kind, and she has learned to drive much more quickly than the average run of girls," adding that the Princess had turned into an "excellent and very considerate driver. She is not rash, and drives with thought for others on the road." To this, the Princess's own instructress, Miss V. Wellesley who served in the 1914–18 war as a motor-cycle dispatch rider in the W.A.A.C., added another tribute: "The Princess drives with consideration and care for her car."

Other A.T.S. girls took a tremendous interest in the Princess's progress. At a Service Club at Manchester one day, one of them, a sergeant-driver, plucked up courage to ask the Queen about her, when the King and Queen were visiting the club.

With some trepidation, the girl waited, thinking perhaps she had presumed too much. But the Queen smiled with real pleasure, and told her "Princess Elizabeth is enjoying being in the A.T.S. very much. She is learning to drive a lorry just now, and she seems to spend most of her time diving underneath it!"—a sidelight on Royal activities that quickly went the rounds of the whole A.T.S.

No favouritism was the rule all through the Princess's course, yet a most careful check of her service log showed she had finished in a shorter time than any other girl in her class, passing out as a fully qualified and competent driver on Saturday, April 14, 1945. She had learned to change wheels, to adjust carburettors, to grind in valves, to de-carbonise an engine, re-time it, and to carry out most kinds of running repairs, pitting her brain for the first time in fair, equal and open competition with other girls—and she passed the test with flying colours.

Out on the roads, the same rule of "no favouritism" applied. "Hon. Second Subaltern the Princess Elizabeth", whose Army number was 230873, had to take her chance with the rest of the road-users, Service and civilian. The former motor-cycle dispatch rider, who had braved all sorts of perils in France driving behind the British lines in 1914–18, accompanied her on all her road lessons.

What she did not know about the vagaries of inexperienced drivers was probably not worth knowing, and, well used to being driven along the roads round and about on No. 1 M.T. Centre, in heavy Army lorries by young women who had only just passed their road tests, she can have had no nerves at all. But even such a perfectly controlled passenger may well have felt certain qualms when the King's daughter insisted, as she did, on going out on the roads like the other girls and driving through the traffic on Bank Holiday Monday, with every available private car on the road to Ascot Races. Clad in her khaki battle dress, the Princess drove calmly through the tangle of civilian and military traffic, handling the camouflaged Army car as easily and confidently as if she had been driving her pony-cart in the secluded empty avenues of Windsor Great Park. No one, outside the officers and staff at the Training Centre, knew that she was on the road, and many a Berkshire constable, holding up the workaday car with its obvious tyro driver and her instructor, to let the "priority" race traffic pass, might well have dropped his controlling arm in surprise had he recognised Princess Elizabeth at the wheel. But no one did recognise her. She drove the car back to the Centre without incident, garaged and cleaned it, and was able to tell the King and Queen an amusing tale of her day of Haroun-al-Raschid adventures.

At that time, I have been told, the conversation at the Royal dinner table at Windsor

*With her officers at the A.T.S. Motor Transport Training Centre, and the Centre's mascot.
Note the Princess's two medal ribbons.*

Castle, whenever Princess Elizabeth was able to join her parents there, tended to centre round sparking plugs, rotor arms, dynamos, crankshafts and so on, a feature which must have been a source of considerable amusement to the King, who has himself been interested in things mechanical to such an extent that more than once in his days as a young officer in the R.A.F. he was chipped for being too "engine-minded".

To the Princess, the greatest day of her whole stay with the A.T.S. was when the King and Queen came to inspect the Centre, and to see her at work. This was not her first experience of a Royal visit from the "other side", for a few days earlier, the Princess Royal had come to the Centre to see how her niece was progressing.

But when her mother and father came, it was the first time she had ever been on the "receiving end" of a visit by Their Majesties. Princess Margaret, who had heard a great deal from her sister about her experiences at the Centre, came with the King and Queen, and looked round expectantly for her sister as she got out of the King's car. But Princess Elizabeth was nowhere to be seen among the group of khaki-clad A.T.S. officers receiving the Royal party. With a ramrod-stiff woman sergeant-major walking in front, the King and Queen went slowly round the centre inspecting the class rooms, the workshops and the rest of the centre. Still there was no sign of the Princess. Then, in one workshop, there was a little group of girls in overalls, leaning over the engine of a camouflaged lorry.

115

The Princess, who is nowadays Commodore of the Sea Rangers, takes an interest in the handiwork of Sea Scouts in the days when she was still a Ranger.

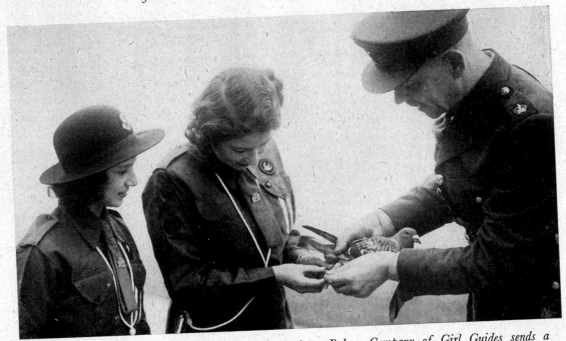

Patrol Leader Princess Elizabeth of the Buckingham Palace Company of Girl Guides sends a "Thinking Day" message to Lady Baden Powell by carrier pigeon on the anniversary of the Scout Founder's birthday.

PRINCESS IN KHAKI

The culmination of her days as a Guide came in March 1945 when it was made known that the Princess had accepted the post of Sea Ranger Commodore of the Girl Guides. This did not mean, however, that she relinquished active association with the movement. Months later, on her first visit alone to Wales, the Princess went to Cardiff to attend and speak at a meeting of the Guides' Council of the Girl Guides' Association for Wales. That night, Princess Elizabeth went up into the hills to the Guides' camp, sat with them round the campfire, and joined in their singsong after supper.

That was one of the last occasions on which the Princess will take part in a gathering of Guides as one of them. When she attended the Guides' parade in Hyde Park just after her twentieth birthday, it was more formally, in her capacity as Commodore, and she stood rightly apart from the other girls, taking the two fingered Guide salute from them as they marched past her. But for a holiday week later in the year, she went again with Ranger friends for training aboard an M.T.B. on the River Dart.

A picture that shows the Princess's perfect teeth: smiling in the uniform of the Sea Rangers, with the badge of "H.M.S. President III" on the sleeve of her jersey, she attends a Sea Scouts Exhibition.

In the Guides, the Princess also met girls from other environments than her own. Though her Kingfisher Patrol companions were mostly daughters of Court officials or of friends of her parents, the crew of the "Duke of York", as her Sea Rangers ship is now called, make up a cross section of the community, and includes a typist, a clerk, a nursemaid, an hotel receptionist, and a groom's daughter.

The Guides' training had fulfilled its purpose. It had definitely added to the equipment, mental, psychological and spiritual, with which the Princess faced the opening of a new life of service, and the Guide law, with its promises to "do her duty to God and the King and to help other people at all times" defines an attitude towards life which she had adopted very much as her own.

CHAPTER EIGHT

"H.R.H. the Colonel"

ON her sixteenth birthday, Princess Elizabeth was appointed by the King to be Colonel of the First, or Grenadier Guards. This was the first fully official appointment under the Crown to be given to the Princess, the other post which she already held, that of President of the Royal College of Music, ranking as a public, but not a Crown, appointment.

To the Princess, this birthday gift was a matter for great rejoicing. It marked a definite stage in her advance towards womanhood and emancipation from the nursery, and she regarded it accordingly with feelings of pride and pleasure, and a determination to do whatever lay within her powers to identify herself with her regiment. To the Grenadiers, also, the King's decision was a matter for rejoicing, for it bound them by yet another tie to the Royal House, and this time to the chief representative of the youngest generation of it, in the person of the heiress-presumptive. At that time, officers and men of the three regular battalions of the regiment, after fighting with the expeditionary force in France as bitterly and hard as ever the regiment had fought in the course of its three hundred years of history, and gaining new glory amid the darkness of Dunkirk, were preparing for a new onslaught against the Germans, with three more war battalions training with them, just ready to go overseas for the start of the long campaign that led them through Africa, Italy, France, Holland and Germany.

With this in their minds, there were not wanting people who, looking at the matter very superficially, thought there was something incongruous in the placing of a young inexperienced girl of sixteen as the titular head of the senior regiment of the world-renowned Brigade of Guards. Such thoughts were strictly confined to people outside the Brigade, who had never taken the trouble to acquaint themselves with its history, for the Princess, though she might be the first woman Colonel of the Grenadiers, was by no means the first Colonel of Royal rank. Nor was the appointment, as some people wrongly supposed, an "honorary" one. True, the Princess could not command the regiment in the field, nor could she reasonably be expected to take an active part in the administrative and training duties of the battalions. But she was, and still is, the actual and active Colonel of the regiment, with clearly defined duties and obligations devolving upon her, duties which, in the four years that have passed since then, she has carried out with careful attention.

To understand this position, it is necessary to know something of the peculiar formation of the command in the five regiments of His Majesty's Footguards, of which the Grenadiers are first, the Coldstream second, the Scots Guards third, the Irish Guards fourth, and the Welsh Guards, created in the 1914–18 war, fifth. In supreme command of the Brigade always is the reigning Sovereign, who is Colonel-in-Chief of each and all the five regiments. Under him are five Colonels chosen from members of the Royal family, and figures of more than ordinary military distinction, each of whom is Colonel of one particular regiment. Thus the Duke of Gloucester is the present Colonel of the Scots Guards, a

The Princess watches the King: she stands "at attention" a little to the rear, as her father takes the salute at a march-past on a summer's day in the Grand Quadrangle at Windsor Castle

Photograph: Fox Photos Ltd.

*The Princess is never microphone shy: here she is addressing a
Guards Parade on the eve of VE Day*

position held by the King before his accession. But the five Colonels do not usually do full time duty with their regiments, which alike in the barracks and in the field, are commanded by an officer who, while holding the rank of full colonel, and wearing the crown and two stars that are the shoulder insignia of that rank, is known as the "*Lieutenant-Colonel Commanding*". Under him, in each of the five regiments, are officers of the rank of lieutenant-colonel, in command of the various battalions. They are always referred to in the Brigade as "the Commanding Officer", never as "the (Lieutenant-)Colonel".

Like most other of the queer-seeming paradoxes in British military nomenclature, this is the result of no mere whim or chance, but marks the continuance in an unbroken tradition of a practice which started when Charles II formed the Grenadier Guards in 1656. In that year, Charles, still in exile, raised a regiment from the gentlemen who had followed him, and called it the "Royal Regiment of Guards". Thomas, fourth Baron Wentworth, who formed and commanded the regiment, found that he had other duties claiming too much of his time to allow him adequately and fully to carry out his duties at the head of the Guards, so he appointed another officer to carry them out in his stead, this officer holding the place of the Colonel while he was away was properly called the "Lieutenant-Colonel", since he "held the place" of the Colonel: and so he has remained through the long line of Colonels stretching from the loyal Lord Wentworth of three centuries ago to Princess Elizabeth to-day.

The Princess's immediate predecessor as Colonel of the Grenadiers was her own great-great uncle, Queen Victoria's youngest son, Field Marshal the Duke of Connaught, who held the post up to his death at the age of ninety-two in 1942. Before him, the Colonel was another Royal soldier, the Duke of Cambridge, last Royal Commander-in-Chief of the British Army, and before him Albert, the Prince Consort. Princess Elizabeth's appointment as Colonel, therefore, far from being ill-fitting to the fame of the incomparable Grenadiers, was exactly opposite, illustrating the intimate and long association of the regiment with the person of the Sovereign precisely at a time when the Grenadiers were giving doughty battle in the name of their King to the King's enemies. And the Grenadiers were proud that the King had shown his confidence in them by giving their Colonelcy to his elder daughter as her first post.

As a mark and remembrance of the occasion, the officers of the regiment subscribed for a presentation to their new Royal Colonel, in the form of a diamond brooch, shaped to represent the regimental badge of the Royal Cipher reversed and interlaced.

Colonel John Prescott, "Lieutenant-Colonel Commanding", had handed Princess Elizabeth the brooch before the parade in the quadrangle of Windsor Castle on her birthday, and she scored her first success as a public speaker when she made a short, unexpected, and entirely impromptu speech of thanks—a charming gesture all the more appreciated because of its spontaneity. Since then, the Princess has worn the diamond brooch in the lapel of her coat and the small gilt flaming grenade cap badge of an officer in her hat whenever she has visited her regiment, or taken part in any function connected with the Brigade of Guards.

One small point about that birthday parade, unnoticed by most observers, is worthy of record. For the first time, as they walked round the lines together, Princess Elizabeth went in front of her father—she, and not His Majesty, the Colonel-in-Chief, was the inspecting officer.

In her "Brodrick" cap, with the Grenadiers badge brooch on her lapel, H.R.H. the Colonel inspects the band of her Regiment at a Windsor birthday parade.

When the Princess attained her eighteenth birthday, the officers of the Grenadier Guards decided to give her another present that would serve to mark even more closely her position at their head. In olden days, the Colonel always had a Colour of his own, though this practice had been allowed to lapse many years before, and the King's permission was sought, and very readily obtained, to revive the old custom by presenting the Princess with a Colour of her own, to be known as "H.R.H. Princess Elizabeth's Colour", and to be mounted whenever the Royal Colonel was present in person. The King took a close interest in the proposal, personally suggesting an alteration in the design, by placing the Princess's monogram embroidered in each corner of the Colour. By the time April 21 came round again, and the tall Guardsmen, spick and span in the khaki battledress they contrived to imbue with a smartness to be equalled nowhere outside the Brigade, were drawn up for the birthday parade in the Grand Quadrangle at Windsor Castle, the Colour had left the embroiderers' hands, and stood, still furled in its case, in the charge of a young officer.

Colonel Prescott saluted the Princess as she went forward alone between the old and the new King's Guard—both on this momentous regimental occasion drawn from the

The Colonel of the Grenadiers inspects her own new Colour: in the Quadrangle of Windsor Castle on her eighteenth birthday.

Grenadiers—to receive her Colour from him. Dressed in a coat of hyacinth blue with a peaked hat in her own "Guards style" the Princess bore herself so well, accepting the Colour with such grace and dignity, thanking the "Lieutenant-Colonel Commanding" with such a friendly smile, that two groups of officers, one Canadian, the other American, who were watching from inside the quadrangle railings, had difficulty in refraining from cheers. As the Princess walked past the ranks of khaki-clad, steel-helmeted Grenadiers, not a Guardsman moved his eyes: but not a Guardsman missed seeing that in the lapel of her coat she wore the diamond badge of the regiment given her two years beforehand. They notice things like that, in the Guards. This time the King remained on the saluting dais, leaving his daughter to carry out her inspection as Colonel on her own.

The Princess's Colour is a reproduction in miniature of the King's Colour of the First Battalion. It measures nineteen inches by twenty-one, and is of crimson silk, with the Crown embroidered in colours and gold thread. It has a gold fringe and a gold and crimson cord and tassel.

It differs from the King's Colour in two respects. The battle honours of the First Battalion are omitted, owing to the smaller size of the Princess's Colour, and in each corner, by the "desire"—according to the official description of the Colour—"of His Majesty, the Colonel-in-Chief of the Regiment, there appears in gold thread, H.R.H.'s monogram, surmounted by her coronet"—an interesting example of the detailed attention which the King pays to all such questions of military and heraldic procedure. The coronets follow a design provided by Garter King of Arms from the coronet that appears on the Royal Warrant of the Princess's Arms.

"H.R.H. THE COLONEL"

Again, it is to King Charles II that we have to go to trace the history of the Colonel's Colour. That monarch decreed that the King's Colour of the First Battalion should be the Colonel's "proper"—or, in the modern phrase, "own"—Colour. He directed that the Colour should be of white silk, with a cross of crimson silk throughout, differenced with the Imperial Crown in gold. Charles's brother, James II, changed this design soon after his accession, ordering that his own Company's Colour, and the Colonel's Colour, should be of crimson silk instead of white. Nearly two hundred years later, the allocation of this Colour to the Colonel of the Regiment was confirmed by Queen Victoria, and in an issue of regimental orders for March 26, of 1885, it is stated: "The Colonel's Colour will always be taken as the Queen's Colour of the First Battalion."

This Colour, it must be pointed out, is entirely different from the Princess's personal standard which is flown to signify her presence on many formal official occasions when her father and mother are not present. Her Colour as Colonel of the Grenadier Guards is also flown to indicate her personal presence, and must not be mounted except when she is on parade. But it is purely a regimental symbol, and is never used on any occasion, military or civil, other than parades or inspections of the Grenadiers.

At Windsor Castle, after the Colour had been presented to the Princess, the King, who never fails to interpret the feeling of a crowd, suggested that it should be carried round for the guests, officers of other regiments, wives, relations and friends of Grenadier officers and men, to see, and Sergeant-Major Douglas proudly carried the new Colour round the quadrangle for everyone to examine, and admire the intricate needlework and embroidery of the Colour, in which complete accuracy of colour was demanded.

With the King and Queen, the Princess inspects her new Colour as Colonel of the Grenadier Guards : on her eighteenth birthday.

In military style coat, the Princess climbs aboard a Comet tank after taking the salute at an R.A.C. passing-out parade at Sandhurst.

One feature of Princess Elizabeth's tenure of the Colonelcy is unique in all the long history of the regiment. Just before she was first appointed, her own cousin, the Princess Royal's elder son, Viscount Lascelles, then eighteen, had joined her regiment—which was also his father's old one—in the ranks as a Guardsman, as no other past or present member of the Royal family had ever done. It was not until November 1942 that he received his commission after he had served the necessary months as a cadet, so that for six months the Royal Colonel had her Royal first cousin serving in the ranks of her regiment as a private, a strange position brought about by the new democratic rules of entry for officers, and one which Charles II could never even have imagined when he first formed the regiment. As an officer, Lord Lascelles fought with distinction in the Italian campaign until he was captured by the Germans outside Perugia, leading a patrol near Monte Corneo in June 1944.

Not only on formal parades in honour of her own birthday, but on many other occasions of different kinds, grave and gay, and in many other ways, the Princess has identified herself with the regiment. Perhaps her greatest moment came quite early in her career as Colonel, when, a week before her seventeenth birthday, she went off on her own for the very first time, to inspect a battalion of the Grenadiers stationed "somewhere in Southern

Command" motoring over to them from Badminton, where she was staying on a short visit to Queen Mary. What made this visit specially exciting for the young Colonel was that the battalion she inspected was a Guards tank battalion, part of that magnificent formation which fought so brilliantly in Holland eighteen months later, the Guards Armoured Division. Existence of such a Division was still a secret, its symbol of a human eye, flanked in the familiar blue-and-red Brigade colours, which the Princess saw adorning each of the line of tanks, and sewn on the sleeve of each Guardsman's tunic, remained to the outside world just another of the many mysterious badges and flashes which they saw but did not understand, and the Princess felt a certain justifiable pride in thus being made free of her first war secret. To show her that, even under modern conditions of war, the Grenadiers did not intend to allow such matters as mechanisation and camouflage to interrupt the regimental traditions of drill and soldierly smartness, the tank crews paraded to receive the Royal Colonel with all the precision of line and movement that has gained them the title of the finest foot soldiers in the world. The whole battalion presented arms in the Royal salute with a simultaneous clash of rifles, which the Princess, standing alone on a dais, acknowledged with a slight inclination of her head, and a smile—the form of military "salute" which she worked out for herself, and has since kept for use on all such occasions.

When the Guards had marched past her to the strain of "The British Grenadiers", officers led the Princess over to inspect the tanks.

Never before had the Guards had any direct connection with these queer pieces of self-propelled armoury, but in the short time since the Armoured Division had been organised, the Grenadiers, at any rate, had contrived to put something of the Guards spirit even into their tanks. Dull and ugly their outsides might have to be with camouflage, but inside the tank, as she peered down through the open turret after clambering up onto the top of one, the Princess could see every item of equipment polished and shining in true Guards style. And, as she drove to lunch in the officers' mess, the Princess noted, with some inward amusement, that the carefully camouflaged staff car in which she rode had been given a high polish till its dull khaki paintwork shone with almost a Motor Show finish. As soon as the battalion went into action, of course, all that polish would be worse than useless, for it enabled the car to be picked out miles away as it caught the spring sunshine. But until that time came, a polished car certainly looked smarter, so polished it, and many of the other staff cars which bore the "Eye" sign, were: and they remained polished until the Division moved to its concentration areas before going overseas.

A year later, in March 1944, the Princess saw more of the Guards Armoured Division at the time when preparations for the coming "D-Day" were at their height. It was her first visit to the invading Army of Liberation, and she was thrilled, as no one who saw them could help being thrilled, at the proud bearing and confident spirits of the troops, among whom none were prouder or more confident than the Guards.

This time she showed that she had evidently been thinking about tanks and their peculiar ways in the interval since her last visit, by asking a young officer in command of a Sherman tank the baffling question, "Which part of the track is stationary when a tank is moving forward?"—a question that has been hotly argued in tank "harbours" before and after battle wherever tanks have fought. Princess Elizabeth told the officer she knew from experience that you can put your foot on the bottom of the track, and prove

Princess Elizabeth, Colonel of the Grenadier Guards, takes the salute.

that it stands still while the tank goes forward, but she wanted to know the scientific explanation of the apparent paradox. Unfortunately—or perhaps fortunately for the officer concerned—the Royal party moved on, and the Princess had to follow her father and mother before her curiosity had been satisfied.

On this tour, the Princess saw another aspect of the Guards' way with tanks, watching the squadrons wheel and form into line and change positions with all the accuracy, though little of the grace, of a detachment of the Royal Horse Guards or the Life Guards on their chargers. She herself, with the King and Queen, was several times a passenger in jeeps and half-track scout cars which took them across the tank-ploughed fields to vantage points to watch the training.

Nearer D-Day, Princess Elizabeth inspected two further battalions of the Grenadiers, bidding them God speed in the great ordeal she knew was just before them: though even the Princess did not know when the invasion was to be launched.

Later on, when some of the Guards had come marching home again, with another series of victories to be inscribed on the regimental colours, the Princess said goodbye to the first of the Grenadier war battalions to be disbanded—the Fifth Battalion, which had fought in the African campaign, and in Italy from Anzio—where the Commanding Officer was killed—onwards. The farewell parade at Wellington Barracks was arranged some time in advance for a particular date in May; and no more appropriate date could have been chosen, for, as it happened, it was on May 7, the eve of VE Day, that the Princess drove through the thronging crowds round the Palace gates to the barracks. Her

The Princess greets the Sergeant Major: the tall figure of the Grenadiers R.S.M. dwarfs his Royal Colonel.

farewell to the Fifth Battalion was therefore her last public appearance before the end of the war in Europe, and when, addressing the parade after a march past, she said, "It is fitting before you disperse you should be able to see victory assured..." she paused, looked up, and smiled at the understatement, knowing that at the Palace her father was still awaiting word from Downing Street to proclaim victory that night or the next.

Since then, the Princess has visited the Grenadiers at training at the Caterham depot where so many good Guardsmen have been made: at Windsor: and at Hawick. She has made all the regiment's interests her own, the welfare of widows of Grenadiers, the Old Comrades' Association, and so on. No call on her time is too much if it is a question of the Regiment, and the Lieutenant-Colonel Commanding is a frequently received visitor in her apartments at the Palace or at Windsor Castle. She likes to be kept informed of all

"EYES RIGHT!"   Another battalion of her regiment salutes the Princess.

that is going on, of awards and decorations won by Grenadiers, and of other regimental matters. When, for instance, she heard that the Ladies' Committee, which looked after the welfare of wives and widows of Grenadiers during the war, was to be disbanded, she insisted on travelling specially to London from Sandringham to attend the final meeting at Wellington Barracks, and to make a presentation herself on behalf of the regiment to the secretary of the committee.

The same night, the Princess went to a private dinner at Claridge's, given in her honour, at which she met some of the senior officers of the other regiments of the Brigade of Guards.

A few days before the great Victory Parade of June 8, 1946, the Princess attended a special parade of the Grenadiers, a parade of the wartime soldiers who had helped to win new renown for the regiment, now lined up with other, older Guardsmen, on the Regimental Remembrance Day, to attend service at Wellington Barracks as members of the Grenadier Guards Comrades' Association, to be inspected by the Princess, to march to the Guards Division Memorial on Horse Guards Parade where their President, Lieut.-General Sir Bertram Sergison-Brooke, laid a wreath, and finally, to march past the Palace, where "H.R.H. the Colonel" stood to take the salute. This meant the giving up of yet another of her few free Sundays: but she made no demur. Her Regiment's claim was paramount.

In days to come, Princess Elizabeth may, and probably will, be appointed Colonel of other regiments outside the brigade: and her Army interests will widen. But to her, no other regiment will ever compare with the Grenadiers, the First Regiment of Footguards, and her own first regiment.

CHAPTER NINE

Her Finances and Household

FROM the age of eleven, when the King's Civil List for the new reign was fixed by Parliament at £410,000 a year, Princess Elizabeth has enjoyed a yearly income of £6,000. On her twenty-first birthday, this sum is increased to £15,000 annually, by a Parliamentary decree passed at the same time as the other resolutions pertaining to the Royal family allowances.

The position of the King and the Royal family in relation to the State, from the financial aspect, is somewhat complicated and but little understood. Most people know vaguely that there is an annual allowance to His Majesty and other members of the Royal family for the purpose of maintaining the dignity of the Crown in worthy fashion. Without knowing anything of the detailed provisions, generally even without any clear idea of the actual amounts involved, they are content to regard this as an annual charge on the funds of the State which is the price the nation pays for the luxury and constitutional advantage of being a monarchy. In a republic, of course, the President must have a salary, and an annual State allowance for the expense of entertainment, upkeep of household, and so on, in addition to which there are the recurring expenses of presidential elections, but critics of the monarchial system on the score of expense conveniently overlook this point. The President of the United States, for example, receives a salary of seventy-five thousand dollars a year, plus an allowance for travelling of not more than twenty-five thousand dollars a year, a total of one hundred thousand dollars, or, at normal rates, twenty thousand pounds per annum, with another three thousand for the vice-president.

In fact, the people of Britain make a profit each year as a result of the nation's financial arrangement with the Royal House. This is brought about by reason of the fact that what are known as the "Crown Lands", now by accepted usage and custom regarded as the property of the nation, are, legally, the property of the Crown, and descend, at each demise of the Crown, to the heir who is the next Sovereign, and who, in a formal declaration, "places unreservedly at the disposal of the House of Commons those hereditary revenues which were so placed by his predecessor . . ." a renunciation of the legal claim on all Crown Lands, which immediately precedes discussion in the House of the question of the Sovereign's Civil List, and which transfers to the nation the immense revenues of such property as the ground on which Regent Street is built, and other equally valuable estates. It was "Farmer George"—King George III—who, in 1760, surrendered the land revenues of the Crown for a fixed annual payment, which was given the slightly obscure name of the "Civil List". At that time, the annual gross value of the revenues was in the neighbourhood of £89,000, with a net return of only £11,000. So hugely have land values swollen in the hundred and eighty years that have elapsed since then, that the annual returns of the Crown Lands were marked in the national revenue and expenditure return for the financial year ended March 31, 1945, as yielding a net surplus of £980,000, a sum reached after deduction for administration, property tax, and other items, from a gross return of £1,911,347. On this showing, a credit balance of over half

*Princesses at play: the Royal sisters at a
jig-saw.*

a million pounds is left to the Exchequer after the whole of the Civil List has been paid.

In this reign, the matter is further complicated, and the cost of the monarchy to the nation further and substantially reduced by the position of the Duchy of Cornwall, whose net revenues in 1936 amounted to no less than £117,604. Until the birth of a son to His Majesty, who automatically would inherit the Duchy, these revenues are vested in the Crown, and by His Majesty's desire, expressed in his message to the House of Commons dated March 10, 1937, the annual incomes of both Princess Elizabeth and the Duke of Gloucester (who receives £25,000 a year) are paid out of these sums. The very substantial balance, again by the King's desire, is made available to reduce the amount payable under the Civil List, a further saving to the British taxpayer of something like £86,000 a year.

Princess Elizabeth's £6,000 a year has, during her minority, been administered for her under the charge of the Keeper of the King's Privy Purse. From it all expenses of the Princess's education and upbringing have been met, and big contributions made to her favourite charities, leaving, presumably, a certain balance which will be hers to use as she wishes when she is of age.

For her personal use, the Princess received only a tiny fragment of her income in the shape of pocket money as a child, in accordance with the Queen's firm belief that the value of money should be learnt early in life. Out of her weekly pocket money, which started at a shilling, and never grew to more than five, the Princess was expected to set aside something each week for national savings certificates, as well as putting a small weekly sum away in the Post Office Savings Bank. Some idea of the simplicity of the Princess's upbringing in this direction can be gained from the fact that when, in 1939, she was taken to the headquarters of the Post Office Savings Bank, in Blythe Road, West Kensington, her own account, produced for her at a moment's notice out of the fifteen million others, showed a credit balance of some thirty-odd pounds only.

When the Princess was shown the typewritten card with the details of her account she smiled, perhaps with some justifiable pride that she had saved so much. Other onlookers in her party smiled, too—but at the contrast between this childish capital "of her very own" and the considerable sum of money being dealt with in her name each year.

While she was still living in virtual seclusion, during her "schooldays", Princess Elizabeth's "household" consisted simply of her governess, Miss Marion Crawford, her nurse-in-chief, Mrs. Knight, and a junior nursemaid. During that period there was obviously no need for a lady-in-waiting or anyone else with official status, since the Princess did not appear in public, and it is not the way of our Royal family to fill sinecure posts to keep up an empty ceremonious dignity, so it was not until three months after her eighteenth birthday that the first appointment to her official household was made.

On July 10, 1944, it was announced that Lady Mary Palmer, the twenty-three year old daughter of Lord Selborne, who had been Minister of Economic Warfare since 1942, had been appointed by the King to be Lady-in-Waiting to the Princess, an announcement which caused even more than the usual rush of baseless speculation about the Princess's future. If the Princess was about to embark on a series of public appearances and to make an increasing number of tours about the country, it was patently necessary that she must have a lady-in-waiting to accompany her, and to arrange programmes and details of her visits. But such simple explanations are rarely enough for the gossips, who at once proceeded to construct a whole array of purely imaginary arrangements for the Princess, of which, they averred, the appointment of a lady-in-waiting was the forerunner. The Princess's life, however, continued on its normal lines, without any of the sudden developments forecast by the gossips, and when ten months later, another announcement from Buckingham Palace made it known that a second lady-in-waiting had been appointed to the Princess's household, in the person of the Hon. Mrs. Vicary Gibbs, a young war-widow who subsequently married the Princess's cousin, Capt. the Hon. Andrew Elphinstone, there was not quite the same stir.

Long and careful consideration was given by the King and Queen to the choice of the two young women who would be their daughter's closest companions. Lady Mary Palmer was not one of the Princess's circle of friends, indeed, they had scarcely known each other before an invitation to spend the week-end at Windsor Castle was sent to Lady Mary by the King and Queen, who wished to have an opportunity of making her acquaintance personally before finally deciding to offer her the post. What steps led to first choice of Lady Mary for a position coveted by a great many young women in Society was not revealed at the time. Members of the Household were asked by the King and Queen to suggest any young ladies whom they thought might be suitable and Lady Mary's name was put forward by the King's Private Secretary, Sir Alan Lascelles. Slim, dark-haired, of medium height, with a quiet attraction and charm, she had done nothing to seek the post. Indeed, she confessed herself most surprised, as well as honoured, when the offer was made. She had already shown herself possessed of one of the principal qualities demanded for the position, that of a serious, responsible outlook on life, by devoting most of her time and energies to the unspectacular task of working at a day nursery. She married, after a few months in the Royal Household, Major Anthony Strachey.

The duties of a lady-in-waiting involve among many other things, daily and uninterrupted attendance at the Palace, and the need for appointing a second lady quickly made itself felt, more especially as personal reasons made it necessary for Lady Mary, who gave birth to a son in August 1946, to absent herself from Court for a while. The same careful consideration as before was given to the question. Again, it was not from the Princess's circle of personal friends that the choice was made. The Hon. Mrs. Vicary Gibbs, daughter of Captain A. V. Hambro, M.P. for North Dorset, and a member of the famous banking family, had been left a widow at twenty-two, with one daughter, when her husband, Capt. the Hon. Vicary Paul Gibbs, elder son of Lord Aldenham, was killed

An unusual picture of the Princess in the Royal car with her mother and sister. She is smiling at the cheering crowds watching her leave Westminster Abbey after an Empire Youth service.

at the head of his men, leading an assault by the King's Company of the Grenadier Guards on the German-held bridge across the River Maas at Nijmegen, in October 1944, an action whose details were well known to the Princess, as Colonel of the Regiment. As in the case of Lady Mary, a friendship and confidence quickly grew up between the Princess and her new lady-in-waiting, whom she calls by her Christian name, Jean.

It was during Mrs. Gibbs' first period in-waiting that the Princess began to go out and about in private, visiting theatres and attending supper parties in the West End. Her lady-in-waiting, of course, accompanied her on all these occasions. Society gossips, concentrating on the Princess, failed to notice that nearly always Captain the Hon. Andrew Elphinstone, second son of the Queen's sister, Lady Elphinstone, who had served in the Cameron Highlanders since 1938, and had been a fellow prisoner-of-war with her other cousin, young Viscount Lascelles, in Germany for many months, was also in the party. It was a surprise, therefore, to the outside world, though not to those within the Palace circle, when on February 27, 1946, an engagement was announced between the Princess's cousin and her lady-in-waiting.

At the end of May 1946, the appointment of a third lady-in-waiting illustrated the growth of the Princess's daily commitments. Lady Margaret Egerton, sister of the Earl of Ellesmere, twenty-eight years old, and an ex-officer of Princess Elizabeth's own service, the A.T.S., took up her duties at once, to allow Mrs. Gibbs time for her wedding preparations. But the Princess's diary by now was so full, her daily post-bag of requests and invitations so heavy, that there was ample scope for three ladies-in-waiting.

Earlier still, the nucleus of the Princess's domestic staff had been formed when she was given a personal maid. For this post, the Queen, whose own maid is a Scot, chose a young Scots woman, Miss Margaret MacDonald, quiet-spoken, red-headed, and unobtrusive.

She has been with the Princess a number of years, probably knows more about her Royal mistress, and says less, than anyone else.

Another question raised at the time of the decision that the Princess should begin her public career was that of her personal security. Constitutionally, it is the responsibility of the Home Secretary to ensure the safety of the persons of the Sovereign and his consort and the heir to the throne, which means, in practice, that the task of guarding members of the Royal family falls to the Metropolitan Police. Hitherto, on the few occasions on which she had gone about without her parents, the Princess had had no special guard assigned to her. The need for a separate police officer to be attached exclusively to the Princess now arose, and the Scotland Yard authorities appointed a tall, clean-shaven sergeant from "A" division, with considerable experience in plain-clothes duties, to this by no means light task. Black-hatted, uncommunicative, the man from the "Yard" sits always in the front of the Princess's car, is near at hand on all occasions, when the Princess goes out of the Palace, whether to an official public function, or to a private theatre party or a dance: and like everyone in her entourage, has a sincere regard for, and admiration of, the Princess.

That, together with a young footman, whose duties include the announcing of official visitors, the summoning of cars, and so on, constitutes the Princess's household to-day. She has no secretary as yet, and the constantly increasing daily correspondence that flows into the Palace addressed to her by all sorts of people from all parts of the world, from mayors of towns desiring her to pay them visits, from the secretaries and committees of societies and institutions wanting her to associate herself with their work, or to attend their meetings, from poor unfortunates, begging her help as a last resort, from well-wishers, from cranks and lunatics, from girls of her own age, and from children of all races, tongues and creeds, is dealt with by her ladies-in-waiting, assisted by a woman clerk who, doing similar work for the Duke and Duchess of York in the old days at Piccadilly, watched the Princess grow up from babyhood.

As the calls on her time and the number of her public duties increase in the next few years, the Princess's household will have to be extended. One or two more ladies-in-waiting are likely to be needed, and the appointment of a male Comptroller of the Household can be foreshadowed. He would be responsible for all arrangements of staff duties and the like, the administration of her finances, and would see to it that the Princess was left free of any concern about the internal running of her household. Up to now, when Princess Elizabeth has fulfilled engagements that have taken her away from the Palace for more than a day at a time, the King has attached one of the senior members of his own household to her to act, more or less, in the capacity of temporary Comptroller, and it may well be from among the younger members of His Majesty's present entourage that the future head of the Princess's household may be chosen. The salaries and expenses of all members of her household and staff are met from the Princess's yearly income.

Though the Princess has had a household of her own since she was eighteen, she has not a house. It may well be some time before she sets up a separate establishment of her own, for the present arrangement, whereby she lives at Buckingham Palace or Windsor Castle with the King and Queen, and yet maintains her own establishment, receiving her own guests, making her own independent appointments, works smoothly and conveniently.

A happy family group, against a background of regal splendour: the King puts one arm round Princess Elizabeth, links the other with the Queen's, while Princess Margaret holds her mother's hand. The Princesses' pet Corgis add a homely touch

Outside her very own house: the six-year-old Princess about to enter " Y Bwthyn Bach ", the " Little House "
given her by the people of Wales.

At present, the Princess has three "homes", one at Buckingham Palace, another at Windsor Castle, and a third at Royal Lodge, the favourite country home of the King and Queen in Windsor Great Park, where they like to live without state, as a private family. At the Lodge, the personal servants who wait on the King and Queen and the Princess discard their Royal livery of blue or scarlet, wear instead the plain black clothes of private service. Here, the Princess has her own room, like the daughter of any well-to-do family. But in the garden, she has a house of her own. This is the famous "Y Bwthyn Bach", "The Little House", given to the Princess by the people of Wales when she was six years old.

Emphatically 'not a doll's house, "Y Bwthyn Bach" was fitted and equipped in every detail as a comfortable modern residence, with running hot and cold water in the rubber floored, blue and white bathroom, a radiogram which works, a grandfather clock in running order, a half-tester bed with pale blue chintz curtains, a portrait of the Queen in the panelled-wood living room, a telephone and all other amenities. But everything was scaled down to accommodate a child of six. Here the Princess used to delight in giving tea parties, to which she would invite only her small friends—no grown-ups could attend, even if they had been asked, which was certainly a great part of the charm of the

An early lesson in telling the time : Princess Elizabeth explains the sundial to Princess Margaret outside her miniature house.

house. Later, when Princess Margaret was six, she took over occasional duty as "hostess". Now that both Princesses are, like Alice when she first found the gold key on the glass table, too big to get in at the door, the Little House is no longer in use, but stands in the King's gardens, a charming memento of the days when his daughters were very young.

Nearby is that piece of garden which was the Princess's own, and which she used to tend herself as a ten-year-old, learning to dig and hoe and rake and cultivate, and, more important still, to clean and put away her tools herself when she had done with them. Such incidental lessons in tidiness were a marked feature of the routine of nursery days, with the result that to-day Princess Elizabeth has ingrained habits of tidiness and an orderly mind.

At Buckingham Palace, where she spends the greater part of her time, the Princess occupies her own suite of apartments on the second floor, known, in the Palace's own geography, as the "Chamber Floor". A lift just inside the Privy Purse Door (the one on the right hand side of the Palace as you look at it from the Mall) gives access to the Princess's rooms, which are in the front, with windows looking out over the Mall and across St. James's Park. There are three rooms, a bedroom, a dressing-room, a sitting-room, and a bathroom, in the suite, making it completely self-contained. Decorations are in tasteful simplicity, with one or two water colours on the walls, and silver framed pictures of the King and Queen and Princess Margaret on the Princess's plain mahogany desk that stands in the centre of the sitting-room. Her telephone is connected through the Palace switchboard in the Court Post Office on the far side of the Palace, and on her desk is a triple bell-push to allow her to summon her lady-in-waiting, her footman or her maid. Though the Palace number appears in the telephone book, outside callers cannot of course ring up the Princess. Palace switchboard operators have a code enabling them to know who may be connected to her extension. These same rooms were formerly occupied by the late Duke of Kent, in his days as Prince George, and before him, by the Princess's father as a young man. They were set aside for Princess Elizabeth's use some time ago, but it is only since the Court took up permanent residence in London again after the end of the war that she has used them. Before that, she shared the "nursery suite" on the same floor, but on the north side of the Palace, with her sister, who now has that suite for herself. When she is in the Palace, the Princess nearly always has family lunch and dinner with her mother and father. If her parents are away and she is alone, she will often have a cold tray sent up for supper. When the King and Queen are entertaining official guests to luncheon, a newly appointed Governor General and his wife, a British Ambassador who has just kissed the King's hands before starting out on his mission, or other people of importance, the Princess is definitely expected to be present at luncheon unless she has official business of her own elsewhere: at other times, she is free to be out to lunch and dinner as she wishes. In this way, the Princess has had already many opportunities for meeting the men at the top of the British diplomatic service, and their wives, as well as scores of other distinguished figures. She has heard and taken part in their conversations with her father and mother, which must have given her considerable insight into questions of state and of high policy. This attendance rule, incidentally, did not apply, or rather,

Even Royal gardeners have to guard against the birds: a happy picture as the Princess adjusts the nets.

applied in reverse, in the case of the weekly luncheons on Tuesdays throughout the war, at which the Prime Minister, Mr. Winston Churchill, was the King's solitary guest. So that the King and the chief Minister of the Crown might have uninterrupted freedom to talk over the highest and closest of war secrets, no one else, not even the Queen, was present, and cold dishes, served through a hatch, overcame the servant difficulty. Of course, at other times, when Mr. Churchill has been the guest of the King, either alone or with Mrs. Churchill, both the Queen and the Princess have been present, and conversations between the heiress-presumptive, with her quick, eagerly inquiring intelligence, and the veteran statesman, with his broad vision and wide perspective of world affairs, were of equal delight to each. When the King and Queen entertained the Empire Prime Ministers to dinner in May 1944, the Princess was taken in to dinner by General Smuts, and sat between him and Mr. Mackenzie King. Occasionally, when her friends are meeting her at the Palace before a theatre party, the Princess asks them up to her rooms for a chat, and perhaps a glass of sherry: but if she wishes to entertain any number of her friends, she asks the King's permission to use one of the bigger rooms, sometimes the Pine Room (whose walls were finished, to the orders of King George V, in bare, unpainted wood) on the floor below, sometimes one of the State apartments on the ground floor.

At Windsor Castle, the Princess has her own suite of rooms, as at the Palace. Situated on the first floor of the Augusta Tower, opposite the Sovereign's Entrance, the suite has been occupied several times before by the heir-to-the-throne. One of the four communicating apartments is furnished for use as an audience chamber, where the Princess can receive and talk to official visitors. Another is used as a study, where the Princess has a large, square-topped desk in Empire style, at which she does a great deal of her writing. Spacious and lofty, the Princess's study is decorated in the formal white and gold style that characterises the official apartments at Windsor, the door backed by an overall full-length mirror. Her windows give onto a lovely vista of the Castle gardens and grounds, with the silver Thames running at their foot.

When, in the future, the Princess decides to move into a house of her own, there should be no lack of choice. Clarence House, in St. James's Palace, where the Duke of Connaught lived for many years, would, for example, make an ideal town residence for her. It has a convenient entrance in Marlborough Gate, and looks out onto the lovely lawns of St. James's. Built on the site of a much older edifice, Harrington House, Clarence House owes its name to the fact that it was constructed as a residence for the Duke of Clarence, afterwards King William IV, Princess Elizabeth's great-great-great-granduncle. It is a two storey building with a portico, and strangely enough, in one of the old Warrant Books in the Lord Chamberlain's Office, it is described as "the Queen's House at St. James's", though there is no record of any Queen having dwelt there. The Duchess of Kent, mother of Queen Victoria, moved to Clarence House from Buckingham Palace in 1840, and continued to reside there until her death twenty-one years later.

If she wishes to have a country house as well, there are several small houses on the Royal estates at Windsor which could easily be made available for her, as was Royal Lodge for her parents. Repeatedly, rumour has assigned the big twenty-five-roomed mansion of Sunninghill Park, purchased by the King in 1945 from the executors of Mrs. Phillip Hill, to Princess Elizabeth for her future use. Actually, the house purchase was negotiated without any thought of the Princess's future. The property, which had been part of the Royal estates in the time of Charles I, was needed to complete the chain of Crown-owned lands surrounding Windsor Castle, and was bought in at the first opportunity.

CHAPTER TEN

Clothes, Coupons and a Coronet

FOR all women, even for those who self-consciously claim to be free from such outworn conventions, clothes have a necessary and important place in life. For a Princess, constantly the centre of observation, watched on her public appearances by all, by many admiringly, by some enviously, by some critically, but by few understandingly, they must be by that much the more important. Should a Princess dress carelessly or untidily, it will be taken as an indication that she may be something less than exact in attention to her duties. Should she dress in anything approaching exaggerated fashion, critics will not be wanting to pronounce her nothing but vain and superficial. To find the right middle channel between these two courses is by no means an easy task, as many Princesses in history could be brought to testify. But that is what Princess Elizabeth has set out to do, and, in a very large measure, has succeeded in doing, in spite of the added difficulties of war-time rationing.

Nothing would be easier for her than to become a leader of fashion for the world. Not very far-sighted British dress-designers have, from time to time, privately expressed their regrets that this has not been made the case, for they point, with perfect truth, to the resounding effect on the sales of British materials and British designs which an all-British fashions-campaign led by Princess Elizabeth would have. But such a scheme, however laudable its objects from the view-point of the Board of Trade, would be anathema alike to the Princess herself and to the King and Queen, all three of whom view with something approaching abhorrence any attempt to make advertising capital out of the Royal family, in any way whatsoever. Princess Elizabeth dresses not to please any group of fashion experts, but in conformity with her own personal taste, which, as it happens, tends to the simple both in style and design.

She favours self-coloured materials rather than ornate or intricate patterns. The line of her clothes is never much in advance of, nor much behind the fashion of the day.

Dark blue, a colour that becomes her fair and delicate colouring to most advantage, is one of her favourites. She is fond, too, of appearing in a dress, coat and hat of an enchanting shade of green, almost the colour of newly opened leaves in spring.

For evening wear, she at first confined herself to the white, or near white shades that are the conventional colours for a *jeune fille*. One evening gown, which she often wears for theatre parties, is of white decorated with sequins, and has wrist length sleeves of semi-transparent material. A pale blue, long-skirted frock, worn with a bolero jacket, is a favourite for dances, and the two dinner frocks in which she most frequently appears when dining out are a cherry red crêpe with long sleeves and a "heart" neck, embroidered with sequins, and a plainly-cut black georgette, livened with touches of scarlet ribbon.

Most people believe firmly that the Queen and the Princess each have special clothing coupons allowed them because of the necessity of their always appearing well dressed. The contrary is the case. Neither Her Majesty nor either of her daughters has received any extra coupons for their clothes. Instead the Queen took the scanty allowance of

The Princess wears a striking new hat trimmed with green ostrich feathers

coupons and the consequent restriction on the purchase of new clothes as a challenge to prove how well dressed a woman could be without having a limitless wardrobe, and without buying a new gown for every occasion. Of course, Her Majesty was in a very favourable position in this respect when rationing was introduced, for she had had a very extensive wardrobe prepared for her Canadian tour with the King just before the war began, none of which had been seen in England. But each and every item in that Royal collection, which the Queen chose with such care for the first Dominion visit of her husband's reign, has been seen a great deal in this country since then, for to-day, seven years after the Canadian tour, Her Majesty is still wearing some of the dresses and costumes made for her then.

This advantage did not, however, lie with the Queen's daughters. Princess Elizabeth was a girl of thirteen when war began, and the seven years from thirteen to twenty-one make as big a difference in Princesses as in other girls, so that her present wardrobe has had to be bought entirely within the period of rationing. It is, in consequence, probably the smallest, most limited collection of clothes that the next-in-succession to a great throne has ever possessed, and the Princess is perhaps the first of her line, with the resources of a vast Empire at command, to wear clothes made from her mother's old ones. Many of the dresses in the Queen's Canadian wardrobe were cut on very full lines, with flounced and pleated skirts, from which enough material could easily be taken to make evening dresses in the present severe styles for the Princess, a fact which does much to explain why she has as many frocks as she has, small though that number is.

By dint of careful, unremitting attention on the part of her maid, and by her own care in wearing them, the Princess makes the most of the limited selection she has. Not long ago, when she was visiting an electricity plant with her grandmother, Queen Mary, the Princess and Her Majesty were each given souvenirs of the occasion, as frequently happens at the end of Royal visits. This time, the souvenirs were of an unusual and severely practical kind, for in the square boxes handed them by the directors of the power company, Queen Mary and the Princess found electric irons of the very latest model, with thumb switches operating a thermostatic control to give varying temperatures for silk, linen, and other materials. Delighted with her present, Princess Elizabeth asked officials to give her full working instructions about the switch gear, explaining that her maid would want to make the best possible use of the device, "because she has so much ironing to do in these days of clothes rationing!"

Looking rather shy : the four-year-old Princess as a bridesmaid to her cousin Lady May Cambridge.

On the Captain's Bridge : a study aboard the cruiser H.M.S. Superb.

Advance planning in the purchase of all clothes is another secret behind the Princess's clever use of coupons. Since she has been making her own choice in the last two years, she has bought coats, dresses and hats of such colours and cuts that they can be worn in differing combinations, so as to give some variety to her appearance at the scores of official engagements she has to fulfil. In those happy, coupon-less days before the war, a Princess who was constantly seen in the same series of two or three dresses and coats would have incurred criticism for dowdiness. To-day, Princess Elizabeth has to face the problem in double. She must try to avoid monotony in her dress, without making her wardrobe seem so extensive as to outstep the bounds of coupons. The skill with which she manages this difficult feat owes much to the early influence of the Queen, who never permitted her daughters to dress extravagantly, even in pre-war days.

Three coats, half a dozen hats, three or four frocks of wool, printed silk, and crêpe, with always immaculate shoes and gloves, are the foundations of Princess Elizabeth's smartness. She has never shown any signs of allowing dress to become an obsession with her, though it is fairly certain that, like other girls of her own age, she would welcome the chance to run riot, just for once, in the dressmakers' salons without having to think of coupon values. Her coats and dresses are chosen deliberately to go with each other, and yet to afford contrasts. For instance, she has a coat of dark wool, drawn together with a link button, and having four flap pockets. This she wears over a print silk dress in bright colours, with a small hat formed of a mass of white flowers. Another wool coat in a light pastel blue, tied with a bow at the waist, and decorated with bow knots on the breast pockets, is worn over a matching wool frock, or over a frock of blue crêpe, with either a wide-brimmed felt hat, a halo hat in felt, or a tight-fitting brimless hat, decorated with a profusion of small vari-coloured flowers. Her most sophisticated hat is a green toque shape, covered with two lovely ostrich feathers, in green and brown, which looks particularly well with her leaf-green coat.

The honour of the Princess's custom is divided between several well-known dressmakers, so that none may claim her exclusive patronage, and, while she is not of age, no tradesmen have been "appointed" to her by Royal Warrant.

Princess Elizabeth had her first long dress at the unusually early age of five and a half, when she made her first official appearance in public at a Royal family ceremony— the wedding of her cousin, Lady May Cambridge, daughter of the Earl of Athlone, and Princess Alice, Countess of Athlone, to Captain (now Lieutenant Colonel) Henry Abel Smith of the Royal Horse Guards, who had been A.D.C. to her father during his term of office as Governor General of South Africa. It was of blue velvet, worn with a Juliet cap, and when, at the fitting, which took place in the Duchess of York's bedroom at 145, Piccadilly, her nurse suggested to the Duchess, as the dressmaker stood by, that the dress could be cut down after the wedding for wear on ordinary party occasions, the small Princess, who had been turning round examining herself with evident pride in her mother's long mirror, immediately looked up to register a strong protest. "Oh, no!" she exclaimed. "I would like it long always!"

But it was a very long time after that before the Princess wore long dresses again. As a girl, she was dressed under, rather than over, her age, and continued wearing ankle length socks until she was well into her 'teens.

Nowadays, tweeds are her favourite country wear, as indeed, they are with both her mother and father. When they walk—as they often do when State duties permit—in the woods of Windsor Great Park, along the paths that ramble round the Royal family's private country home at Royal Lodge, the King and Queen and both Princesses are nearly always dressed in tweeds. Princess Elizabeth's most recent country suit is of cherry red and grey woven into a Scottish border design in a tweed specially made for her use some months ago by a merchant in Galashiels, who had supplied previously, tweeds for her use as a young girl—and to whom the Princess, this time, sent the regulation fifteen and three-quarters coupons required.

In the Princess's rationed wardrobe there is an item which most British women will envy her, a pair of lovely evening stockings in nylon. They, too, like the electric iron, were a gift to her at the end of a tour of inspection, this time of a big stocking factory, where, again, she was accompanying her grandmother, who was also given a pair of the new stockings. The Princess was frankly delighted with her pair, and did not hesitate to say so. Queen Mary, too, was pleased, but holding up the sheer, light-coloured stockings to the window, permitted herself to remark with a smile, "They look as though they might be rather cold to wear!"

These two pairs of stockings were among the very first to be made of nylon in this country. They were, the factory officials explained to their Royal recipients, really in the nature of experimental products—but that did not render them coupon free, and both Queen Mary and the Princess promised to send the necessary three coupons each when they reached home. Actually, in this case they did not have to part with their own coupons for their unexpected and unasked gift. Instead a woman who had accompanied the party round the factory nobly volunteered to sacrifice six of her own precious coupons on their behalf—an example of twentieth century devotion to the Royal family that is almost worthy to rank beside the famed and somewhat similar sacrifice of Sir Walter Raleigh, when he cheerfully ruined a new and costly doublet to save Queen Elizabeth from walking through the mud.

Yet another gift which came to the Princess without causing any diminution of her remaining clothing coupons, this time with no self-sacrificing aid from anyone else, was a pair of Belfast linen handkerchiefs presented to her during her tour of Ulster in March 1946. Clothing rationing applies just as much in Northern Ireland as anywhere else in the United Kingdom, and women's handkerchiefs, be they of Belfast linen or Egyptian cotton, still require coupons. But in Ireland, even in what is sometimes called the "hard North" they take a different, more romantic, view of such events as a Royal visit. To ask Her Royal Highness for a coupon in exchange for a gift? It was unthinkable to the generous loyal Ulster mind, and so no question of coupons was raised as the two pretty Irish girls, all smiles and blushes, handed a sample of their work to the Princess in the roadway on that fine spring morning. If the donors of the handkerchiefs were not concerned with the matter of coupons, no one else in Northern Ireland felt they need be; and if, now that the story has been made public, there should come a demand from some meticulously-minded official at the Board of Trade for the missing coupons, I am quite sure there would be scores of Ulstermen—and women—eager to give up their coupons for the Princess.

There are two fur coats in the Princess's wardrobe, one of summer ermine, a lovely garment, each skin regular and perfect, and exactly matched in shade. With a small collar and narrow lapels, it is shaped to her figure, small-waisted, and three-quarter length. The other is of white ermine, a very smart evening wrap, which she wears to dances, dinner parties, and other formal evening functions.

Two universally accepted canons for good dress, which apply equally to men and women, are never to wear clothes that are *outré* or sensational, always to wear clothes that are suited to the occasion. On both of these scores, at least, Princess Elizabeth can certainly claim to be well dressed. Sensational clothes have never made any appeal to her. There is no reason why they should, since she is apt always to be the most looked-at person in any assembly, and therefore has no need to call attention to herself. Even in the matter of hats, she is of conservative taste, preferring plainly styled models, with rarely any great ornamentation, beyond the spray of light flowers that seems her favourite.

As far as the second canon is concerned, the clothes the Princess took with her on her first sea voyage unaccompanied by her mother and father, when she crossed from Greenock to Belfast in the 9,700 ton cruiser, H.M.S. *Superb*, are a sufficient indication of her good sense of what is fitting. For the formal reception aboard the warship, where all the ship's company were lining the deck, the Royal Marines band playing the National Anthem on the quarter-deck, while a guard of honour of Royal Marines gave the Royal salute as she joined the ship, Princess Elizabeth wore a charming outfit of dark blue, her fur coat, and a dainty hat of matching blue, finished with a high bow in contrasting shades of blue in the front and an off-the-forehead veil of blue net. She wore shoes of dark blue leather, with semi-high heels. The whole ensemble was so exactly right for the occasion that it provoked favourable comment from the spectators who saw her embark, from the officers of the *Superb*, and, more significant still, even from those notoriously hard-to-please observers, the lads from the lower deck. So far, so good, but the Princess had announced her intention of going up on the bridge during the crossing and, with a gale warning just received (some well-disposed lover of Royalty in the office of Aeolus, God of the Winds, must have changed the Orders of the Day at the last moment, for the threatened ⸘gale turned away to the north-west just before it should have met the ship) a hat with a high bow did seem likely to be troublesome rather than very comfortable. The arrival of the Princess on the bridge was, therefore, awaited with considerable interest.

With the Captain of Superb, Captain H. W. S. Sims Williams, she watches the course ahead.

When she came up from the Captain's cabin, which had been put at her disposal for the passage, Princess Elizabeth had changed her attire completely. In place of the smart fur coat, she wore a belted camel hair coat that had obviously seen some service: her stylish hat had been replaced by a gaily coloured silk scarf knotted under her chin, her shore-going shoes by a flat-heeled, soft, comfortable-looking pair of blue suede edged with white, her blue costume by a jumper and skirt. It was an outfit just as suited and proper to the occasion as the other had been, with the result that, as she sat in the captain's high wooden chair on the starboard side of the bridge, looking at the widening banks of the Clyde while the *Superb* steamed down river, she fitted charmingly into the picture, looking, and undoubtedly feeling, perfectly at her ease. The Navy, no mean judges, chalked up a definite mark in favour of Princess Elizabeth then and there.

That camel hair coat and head scarf are the Princess's usual outdoor "off-duty" wear if she is going out for her usual morning stroll round in the grounds of Buckingham Palace with her sister and their dogs, or taking a walk or a canter in Windsor Great Park. Quite often, she discards the scarf to leave her head bare. A dark blue hand-knitted jumper and a blue skirt are among her other preferences for morning informal wear.

Just how quickly and directly Princess Elizabeth's influence is reflected in the fashions of the day is shown by the story of the peaked military-style hat she wore for her first inspection of the Grenadiers on her sixteenth birthday. The Queen had decided that, notwithstanding the precedent of Queen Victoria, who wore, according to contemporary accounts, "the uniform of a Field Marshal"—details are, unfortunately, not specified—when she reviewed 18,000 soldiers at the new Aldershot Camp after the Crimean War, and semi-military uniform, with a buttoned tunic and pill-box hat, when she reviewed the Volunteers in Hyde Park, the Princess should not wear either uniform or anything that looked like a travesty of it. But the question remained of what clothes the young Royal Colonel should wear, which would combine the advantage of being wearable on other occasions, and yet not look out of place at a military parade. The solution was found in a plainly-cut coat of green cloth, with a flat, brimless hat of green felt, shaped somewhat on the lines of a "Brodrick"—the ordinary flat peaked cap of our soldiers, named after Mr. John Brodrick, the Secretary of War who designed them—entirely bare of ornament, like a Brodrick, with a deep peak in front. It was a happy choice, which gave just the needed semi-military touch. Next day, pictures of the Princess were widely published, with captions calling attention to her new hat fashion. Within a few hours, Mayfair hat shops were receiving urgent orders from women eager to have the first copies of the "Princess's cap", and in the matter of weeks, the peaked caps appeared on the heads of women all over the country.

Two other examples of the Princess's clever aptness with clothes were also seen at military inspections. One was the beret-shaped hat she wore at a parade of the Grenadiers in 1945. It was trimmed only with a wide band of plain, matching ribbon, but the ribbon was deftly formed into a representation of the flaming grenade that is the regimental cap badge. The other was in the cut of the new coat she wore at a Sandhurst inspection, again, of course, a military occasion. The Princess had the coat cut with a double-breasted front, wide lapels, and the same smart waist and shoulder line of a Guards greatcoat. It gave her a military air, without looking in the least as if she were aping uniform. Simply recorded, these ideas seem obvious enough, but they do show that the Princess devotes a good deal of thought and attention to her choice of clothes.

It will surprise most people to learn that Princess Elizabeth has no State robes of her own. She is not, of course, a Peeress of the Realm, so she could not, even if she wished, claim, as have some of the select band of peeresses in their own right, permission to wear the robes of red silk, slashed with bars of ermine to indicate their degree, such as are worn by the peers on State occasions like the opening of Parliament; and there are no provisions in existence for State or ceremonial robes for the eldest daughter of a Sovereign, even though she be heiress to the throne as well. When Queen Victoria went for the first time to dissolve Parliament, only a few weeks after she had acceded to the throne, and before her coronation, she wore an ermine-lined mantle of crimson velvet, an ermine cape, a white satin robe, richly ornamented with gold, a diamond tiara and stomacher, and the blue ribbon and diamond insignia of the Garter, her full robes of State as a Queen as yet uncrowned. Two months earlier, she had, like Princess Elizabeth to-day, possessed no formal robes to mark her position as Queen-to-be.

This absence of ceremonial wear for the Sovereign's heir caused some deep thought at Buckingham Palace early in the King's reign, when a request came from a certain native colony of undoubted loyalty for a photograph of the Heiress-presumptive in her Royal robes as a Princess. A diplomatic way was found round the request, by the dispatch of a picture of the Princess in a family group, with the explanation that she was as yet too young for official photographs to be taken of her alone.

Princess Elizabeth was the first female heir to the throne in memory to attend her father's coronation, which robbed those responsible for the planning of the ceremony of the guidance of precedent, and caused some extra worries in the household of the new King and Queen, who had, amid all their other problems, to decide on what their two daughters should wear. There was some discussion whether distinction should be made between the two sisters' dresses to indicate their differing places in the line of succession. Originally, it was proposed that only Princess Elizabeth should wear a train: but at this news, the story went at that time, Princess Margaret, aged six and a half, staged what we would now call a "sit-down strike" and refused to take any further part in Coronation rehearsals or training, until her father had given instructions that she, too, should have a train.

Princesses in pantomime

QUEEN OF TO-MORROW

At the great service in Westminster Abbey on May 12, 1937, both Princesses were dressed alike in white lace frocks of ankle length, with white socks, white satin slippers, and ceremonial robes of Royal purple, attached to their shoulders by gold tassels, with a waist length cape of ermine hanging between the shoulders. Neither wore the velvet kirtle, which is part of the ceremonial robe of a peeress.

Each Princess wore a golden coronet, to signify their rank as the sovereign's daughters, and these coronets, specially made for that one great occasion, have never been worn again.

Princess Elizabeth will in fact never wear hers on any other occasion. When she attends the opening of Parliament with her father, one of the few ceremonies at which the King wears his Crown, or even in the unlikely event of her opening Parliament on his behalf, she would wear nothing more than a diamond tiara, for the rule is that Princesses wear coronets only at a coronation, and the only other coronation the Princess is likely to attend is that at which she would herself be the central figure on whose head no coronet, but the Crown Imperial itself is set. Princess Margaret thus has a chance of wearing her coronet again—but as she was not quite seven when her father was crowned, it is probable that a new, and larger circlet of gold would be required!

Even for the Princesses' coronets at Coronation time, no exact precedents could be found. The Princess Royal had, it is true, attended the Coronation of her father, King George V, but then she was neither next nor next but one in succession. So new coronets had to be designed for the King's daughters. Inspired by the thoughts of regal magnificence that hovered in the pervading air of those days, so filled with majestic ceremony, the men charged with this difficult task evolved two striking coronets of gold, lined, as is the King's crown, with crimson velvet, and broidered with ermine. But when the coronets were taken to Buckingham Palace for the Princesses to try on, neither the Queen, nor Queen Mary, whose sage advice had been asked by the King and Queen, cared for them in the least. They looked, it was felt, too much like a stagey imitation of the real crown. That would not do at all. So away the coronets were taken, and down the designers sat to do some quick thinking, for time was getting short, and Coronation Day loomed increasingly nearer. The essence of their problem was to produce a coronet that was regal, yet not too ornate to be worn with dignity by two girls of eleven and seven. It was, I believe, Queen Mary who hit on the solution, by asking the designers to think simply, what do children wear when they are playing Kings and Queens? A simple circlet of gold (actually, time was so short that gilt metal had to be substituted) was the answer, but even now there was yet another pitfall for those who made the coronets. As Princess Elizabeth of York, the Princess would have worn the strawberry leaves indicating her father's rank as a Duke and in the first sketches of the revised design, the strawberry leaf was incorporated in the design.

When the King saw this, he at once struck out the strawberry leaf motif, which was no longer correct. As befits one who is the "Fountain of Honour", the King insists on a punctilious observance of all the rules of heraldry in all matters concerning his own family, and, judged heraldically, to include strawberry leaves in the design was all wrong, for the Princesses were now no longer of York, but of England, their father no longer a Duke, but the King. Once more, the designers started from scratch, the coronets were finished with only a few hours to spare, and taken to the Palace where, this time, they gained the King's full approval. The final design was of cross-pattee and fleur-de-lys, both emblems which occur in the ornamentation of the King's Imperial Crown. The coronet incorporated in the Princess's arms (pictured facing page 64) is a replica of the design.

After the Coronation the two coronets were put away with other Royal treasures and souvenirs of the day for safe keeping, and there they remain to this day.

A close up of the Princess in her coronet, with her mother and grandmother after the Coronation.

CHAPTER ELEVEN

Princess in Wartime

BEHIND THE SECURITY "BLACKOUT"

BOTH Princess Elizabeth and her sister were at Balmoral when war broke out. The King, who had already once interrupted his summer holiday to review the Reserve Fleet in Weymouth Bay at the beginning of August, had been called to London again, to stay in his capital while his Cabinet Ministers and his Ambassadors waged their last desperate, unavailing fight to save peace. The Queen went South, too, on August 28, to be at the King's side as the uneasy balance slowly tipped to war. For the first fortnight of that strange unreal first period which did not seem to be war she stayed with the King, then returned to Balmoral for a week to make arrangements for her daughters' mode of wartime living. But the call of greater duty as a Queen and a wife took her back to the King in London, to remain at his side for the rest of the war.

To their own unconcealed delight, the Princesses remained at the Castle, "in residence" alone for the first time in their lives. As the senior member of the Royal family present, thirteen year old Princess Elizabeth assumed the dignity of "head of the household", for, though there were members of the Royal entourage, one of the Queen's Ladies-in-Waiting, her Comptroller, the late Admiral Sir Basil Brooke, as well as Miss Crawford and Mrs. Knight, the nurse, in charge of the Royal sisters, nevertheless it was Princess Elizabeth who was the titular head of the Castle household, a circumstance that had an amusing sequel some three weeks later when the national registration for identity cards was made on Friday, September 29, 1939. Forms had to be filled in at Balmoral Castle, just as in every other house in the land, and in the list of inhabitants of the Castle on that night, the name of Princess Elizabeth was entered in its proper precedence, at the head of all the others, with that of her sister, Princess Margaret, second. All identity cards were numbered in exact accordance with the particulars given in each household with the result that both Princesses hold cards whose numbers start with the letter "S" denoting that the holders are registered in Scotland.

In Princess Margaret's case, this is particularly apt, since she was born in that country. But what pleased young Princess Elizabeth more than the "S" at the beginning of her number was the figure "1" which terminated it—official proof and recognition of her proud position as (temporary) head of the household.

In the remote safety of the Highlands, where, if anywhere, they could be considered safe from the as yet unfulfilled threat of bombing, the two Princesses stayed, leading a quiet uneventful life, for nearly four months after that day on which they had listened first to Mr. Neville Chamberlain, the Prime Minister, telling the world that Britain was at war, and then to the well-known, familiar voice of their own father, warning his people of the great trials to come, and praying for God's help and guidance. They did their lessons, as they would have done at peace, they went for long walks and rides in the Highland countryside where they had spent so many happy holiday hours, and war must

The Sea Ranger Princess: a study of H.R.H. in the uniform of the organisation of which she is now Commodore

Photograph by The Hon. M. W. Elphinstone

Princess Elizabeth meets American ambulance drivers at a "stand-down" parade at Buckingham Palace when the service was disbanded after five years service.

have needed only the encouragement of a Royal example to turn the drift, which was already perturbing the Government, into a flood, with the total collapse of the entire evacuation scheme. The Queen, who knew what fears were in the minds of the King's Ministers, did her best by precept as well as practice to keep the children away in safety. When she went among the people, she made no secret of her regret at seeing so many children back in the towns, and voiced her earnest hopes that the mothers would try to keep them out of danger—a plea that was much the more effective when the Queen could add from her very own experience, "I know how sad it is to be apart from the children: but it's best for them."

Meanwhile, preparations for ensuring the safety of the King and Queen themselves in the event of mass bombing of London had been hurried forward. In the ancient dungeons of Windsor Castle, deep underground, thick stone walls had been strengthened, sturdy roofs, built centuries before, had been buttressed, and a series of air raid shelters constructed that were as safe, even against a direct hit, as anything could be. No one knew what might happen in France, the whole war situation might alter without warning: and Balmoral, five hundred miles away, was not a good place for the heiress to the throne and her sister to be if the disaster which some far-sighted folk predicted came to pass.

So the Princesses travelled south in great secrecy to join their parents for the first Christmas of the war and to take up those quarters at Windsor Castle which were to be their permanent home for the rest of the five years of war.

So well-kept was the secret of their journey that most people in Britain had little if any idea of the Princesses' whereabouts, a fact which the enemy propaganda machine was quick to seize on in an effort to spread dissension.

While the B.B.C. and the home newspapers preserved a complete silence about the Princesses, their names were blazoned out daily on the Hamburg Radio and the other stations operated by Dr. Goebbels and his henchmen, who proclaimed with growing conviction that the King and Queen had sent their daughters out of the country to Canada —a sure sign they added gloatingly that all was over as far as the United Kingdom was concerned.

So persistent and emphatic was the enemy about this, that many people in this country came to believe his story was true, even if they did not let the Princesses supposed absence unduly depress their spirits, or affect their faith in ultimate victory. If the Princesses *had* gone to Canada, most people thought, it was a wise move to ensure their safety as the two next in line of succession; and they were content to leave it at that. Striking proof of the power of Dr. Goebbels' lies came to the present writer one day when five different people, all in positions of some responsibility, assured him that the Princesses had arrived in Canada some days beforehand: which struck him as somewhat strange, in view of the fact that at Buckingham Palace that morning, he had seen both Princess Elizabeth and Princess Margaret on one of their rare brief visits to London. But the overriding need for security prevented evidence of that rebutting kind from being made public. Down at Windsor, the loyal inhabitants of the Royal Borough, accustomed to seeing the two Princesses on their frequent riding or driving excursions through the town, smiled at the German stories —but kept silent.

Plans, very definite, detailed, and elaborate had, in fact, been made with the approval of the Cabinet and the military high command, for the evacuation of the Princesses if invasion should come. Exactly how and where they were to be taken remains an undisclosed "top-secret". At least two big houses in the country, well towards the West, had been earmarked as headquarters for the King if London were to be imperilled or to fall, and his Government forced to quit Whitehall.

The safety of the Royal family if the Germans landed was a problem of paramount importance. Mr. Churchill and the members of his War Cabinet gave the matter their closest attention, and drew up a series of schemes, designed to meet different contingencies. The safety of the Crown itself, the Sceptre, the Orb, and the other jewels of the imperial regalia, then lying hidden deep underground in a specially constructed, air-conditioned vault, at Windsor, whose exact whereabouts was known to fewer than half a dozen people, was also taken into account, and the Cabinet master plan provided for their removal and disposal in such a way that there could be no chance of their falling into enemy hands.

Already, the King was using a splinter and bullet-proof motor car for his daily travels about London. Officers of the Household Cavalry, traditionally charged with responsibility for guarding the King's person in battle, took over control of this car. If the King was not actually in battle, there was certainly the constant threat of enemy attack, as well as

Walking between tanks at a Royal Armoured Corps O.C.T.U.
at Sandhurst

the continual danger from bombing, and the Royal Horse Guards and the Life Guards asserted their right to be His Majesty's immediate protectors. It was from the Household Cavalry and the Guards, therefore, that the small band of trusted officers and men were drawn for "special duty" with the King. Standing by night and day, they were charged with carrying the Cabinet's plans into immediate effect. The officers had been made privy to the secret routes mapped out for the King and his family, had studied them on maps, driven over them, become so familiar with them that they could find their way under any conditions. Cars, their tanks full, their engines in race-track condition, stood in readiness, bearing secret code signs giving them absolute priority over all traffic: and Princess Elizabeth and Princess Margaret were ready at a moment's notice to leave with the King and Queen.

Had these plans been put into effect, the Princesses would have stayed with the King and Queen for a time at least. If the situation had worsened, there was another plan for their evacuation from the country to Canada, where, perhaps, the King and his Government might have had to follow them if the island fortress had fallen. But Hitler's men did not land, the plan did not have to be put into operation, and the Princesses continued to live happily at Windsor.

Here they were to stay, with but brief intervals, for the rest of the war. Security needs still reigned supreme, and the British public was not allowed to know—however many people may have guessed—where the Princesses were. All references to them were cloaked in the semi-secrecy of the phrase "a house somewhere in the country", under which ignoble anonymity Windsor Castle had to remain till peace returned.

Princess Elizabeth spent six wartime birthdays at the Castle. It was there, as has already been recorded in these pages, that she was made Colonel of the Grenadiers, there that she came of Royal age at eighteen, there that she signed her first State papers as a Councillor of State while her father was abroad, but not until her twentieth birthday, in the first full year of peace, could it be announced in advance where she would celebrate the anniversary. In the war years, a handful of privileged guests at the quiet ceremonials within the Castle, or at most a few hundred of the Windsor townsfolk, had greeted her on her birthdays. By contrast, on Easter Sunday, April 21, 1946, thousands of loyal citizens made their way to Windsor for the holiday, eager to see, most of them for the first time, the heiress to the throne. By the King's permission, the East Terrace of the Castle, which runs underneath the windows of the Royal apartments, was thrown open to the public, and two Guards bands, those of the Royal Horse Guards, and of the Princess's own regiment, the Grenadiers, played in the afternoon. As a result, an astonishing display of enthusiasm occurred, with over thirty thousand people crowded in orderly fashion along the Terrace, cheering lustily at every interval in the music, as they looked up to the open windows of the Royal rooms, where Princess Elizabeth sat with the King and Queen, Queen Mary, and Princess Margaret. It was a remarkable demonstration of popular affection for the Princess and her parents, the first opportunity the country had had of showing its feeling for the young Royal heiress. No particular significance attached to this anniversary as had to her eighteenth birthday, beyond the fact that the Princess was saying goodbye to her 'teens, but the crowds cared nothing for that, content and delighted at the good fortune that had brought her birthday to coincide with Easter Day, giving them freedom to go and cheer her.

One hundred and nine years earlier, another heiress of England, Princess Victoria, celebrated her important eighteenth birthday, the last she was to spend as a Princess, at Kensington Palace. The day was observed as a public holiday. At six o'clock in the morning, the Union Jack was broken on the tower of Kensington Church. Then another flag floated out. On this banner of pure white silk was embroidered in what all writers of the time agree in calling "ethereal blue" the name "Victoria". Some minutes later, the gates of Kensington Palace gardens were opened to the public, and early risers crowded in to hear a birthday serenade played and sung to the Princess "by thirty-seven vocal and instrumental performers, led by Mr. Rodwell, Composer to H.R.H., and Mr. J. Weippert, Her Royal Highness's harpist". From her window, the Princess heard an ode, *Victoria's Natal Day*, beginning "Wake, Royal maiden, from soft repose, As zephyr awakes the unfolding rose . . ." and from eight o'clock onwards, church bells rang at intervals in honour of the day. Both Houses of Parliament observed the holiday, and that night thirty-eight public dinners, each attended by a Member of Parliament, were held, "within four hours' ride of the metropolis."

One M.P., presiding over the banquet at Kensington, stressed, as even the most loyal of Parliamentarians was apt to do in those days, that the acclamations with which her "coming of age" had been greeted were the homage of a free people, of men who knew their own rights and who were prepared on all fitting occasions to maintain them: but they were also prepared to render due respect and to tender the fullest and most loyal affection to the Sovereign. The concluding sentences of that century-old speech could be repeated without alteration to-day. "When, in the fullness of time, the illustrious Princess is called upon to ascend the throne of her ancestors, she will, I am in my heart confident of it, obtain that best title to the Crown, the confidence, the respect, and the affections of the people."

The comparison between those rather over-formalised rejoicings of Victoria's day, that savour a little too much of stage management, and the spontaneous, unrehearsed enthusiasm of the Easter crowds on Princess Elizabeth's latest birthday, to say nothing of the almost complete absence of ceremony on her eighteenth anniversary, is a comparison between the two ages. Imperious Victoria, even at the end of her long reign, could little have foreseen, nor would she probably much have relished, the days when the Sovereign's greatest active daily power is exercised by force of example, when the King is regarded more and more as the trustee and guardian of his people's right to their own independent democratic rule: but the warm-hearted affection of the Easter crowds for her great-great-granddaughter would have brought her real joy. It was evidence, if evidence were needed, that no matter what the changes in the political scene, no matter what further brakes a flexible constitution might put on the powers and prerogatives of the Throne, the country's love for the monarchy had not changed, but had strengthened, and become more personal with the passing of the years.

Of all the happenings at Windsor Castle during the war years, the events that immediately preceded Princess Elizabeth's sixteenth birthday would have caused Queen Victoria most surprise. On that day, the Princess, accompanied by her mother, set out from the Castle in one of the royal cars, to drive to Victoria Street, where the big maroon limousine halted outside an unpretentious entrance, above and beside which several printed notices bearing the King's name were displayed. It was the local Windsor

Office of the Ministry of Labour, more familiarly known as the Labour Exchange, and the King's daughter went there, as 20,000 girls of her own age were doing all over the country at their local exchanges, to register under the National Service Act, on reaching the age of sixteen.

That procedure had been decided upon by the King for more than one reason. For the Princess to register "at home", at Buckingham Palace or Windsor Castle, would have been to give her a privilege denied to all other youthful candidates for national service: for her to have gone to the Ministry of Labour, and filled in her form in the presence of

She takes her duties as Colonel of the Grenadier Guards very seriously. Here she is greeting wounded officers of the Regiment.

Mr. Ernest Bevin, then Minister of Labour, would have seemed too much like showmanship, and this above all was what the King wanted to avoid. Besides these negatives, there was the positive advantage that if the Princess went to the local Labour Exchange, it would do much to remove the snobbish reluctance of many parents to let their children visit the Exchanges, which, until then, had been largely associated in the public mind with unemployment and the "dole".

When Princess Elizabeth, in the uniform of her own "pre-entry" training organisation, the Girl Guides, walked into the little, sparsely furnished Exchange where two girl clerks

"Jimmy" Doolittle, Commanding General of the Eighth U.S. Army Air Force, tells the Princess what his planes have been doing, at an American airfield "somewhere in England".

and she met, besides, all the Empire leaders who came to Britain, General Smuts, the elder statesman of Empire, Mr. Mackenzie King of Canada, Mr. Curtin of Australia, and Mr. Peter Fraser of New Zealand, as well as the chief representatives of the Allies who came here, among them Mrs. Roosevelt, who was her parents' guest at Buckingham Palace.

Apart from these personal contacts with the men and women at the top, who were directing, in greater or less measure, the whole course of the war, the Princess had no "inside information". She was not at any time allowed access to the secret papers of State, with the single exception of the short time when, in the absence of the King in Italy, she acted as one of the Councillors of State, nor did she ever know the contents of the confidential dispatches which constantly arrived at all hours of the day and night for her father's attention whether he was "on duty" in London or "on leave" at Windsor, and she kept her own maps of the various fronts, marking the Allied and German lines in accordance with what she read in the newspapers and heard on the wireless. Perhaps the King, who knew the real truth of the position at all times, good or bad, may have smiled to himself if he happened to see his daughter's maps when—as in the early stages of the Normandy invasion—the paramount need for keeping the enemy in ignorance decreed that the public at home must also be a little misled. But he certainly never ventured to alter any of the markings.

One of the earliest big thrills of the war for Princess Elizabeth was when she achieved what was, at that time, the ambition of nearly every boy and girl in the country by going aboard an aeroplane of the Royal Air Force. It was a twin engine Hudson aircraft of Coastal Command which the Princess climbed aboard one winter's day early in 1941, when she and her sister Princess Margaret went with the King and Queen to Bircham Newton aerodrome, the nearest R.A.F. station to Sandringham. Incidentally, it was not from Sandringham that the Royal party drove. During the war, the King closed his big house in Norfolk, using instead the smaller, nearby Appleton House, which had belonged to Queen Maud of Norway. It was the first time either Princess had been to a R.A.F. station at war, and everything they saw was an excitement. But the best moment came when the Station Commander, having first obtained the King's permission, asked the two girls if they would like to see the inside of one of the planes. Almost before the plane door was open, the Princesses had clambered up onto the fuselage, and a moment later were inside the aircraft, examining the controls, asking rapid-fire questions about speeds and heights and U-boat attacks. Princess Elizabeth sat in the pilot's seat, handling the controls herself, while Princess Margaret lay down flat to bring an imaginary enemy into the bombsights.

Afterwards, the Princesses stood by as the King and Queen met pilots and crews and heard first-hand tales of lonely patrols over the sea, of chases after submarines, of the rescue of survivors of their attacks. They saw a novice pilot being coached in a "link-trainer" watching the blind course "flown" by the pilot as it appeared on the recording table, then they saw planes taking off for and coming in from routine searches for the enemy, ending their afternoon by having tea with the King and Queen in the officers' mess.

That was an isolated occasion, an after-Christmas outing for the Princess and her sister. It was not to be repeated for another three years, and Elizabeth went back to her studies at Windsor, content to help on the war effort in such little ways as she could, aiding in the local salvage drive, growing vegetables and fruit in her garden at Royal Lodge, knitting comforts for the Forces. She was a constant listener to the B.B.C. news bulletins, and to the French transmissions in the European Programme. How often, if at all, she listened to the sublimely unconscious humour of the traitor-broadcasts of Lord Haw-Haw is not recorded, but she certainly was a devotee of his imaginary compatriot "Funf" in the early Itma programmes, to which, as she subsequently told Tommy Handley, she and most of the Royal family at Windsor, including the King, listened with great glee.

At Windsor, too, the Princess, like other young people, learned the drill of fire fighting, practising stirrup pump exercise with her father, familiarising herself with the raid alarm procedure, and so on. She became quite expert, too, in aircraft recognition.

It was not until the Allies' "Invasion Year"—1944—that the Princess began to go about among the King's forces with her father and mother—except, of course, for the military visits to her own regiment she made as Colonel of the Grenadier Guards. Then, the King decided that with such epochal history in the making whose outcome must govern the shape of the world to-morrow, it was only fitting and right that his daughter, who on some morrow, near or distant, would be called into the midst of world affairs, should see something of the mighty events that were in process of formation. Also, there was the thought that the troops, about to set off on the greatest of all adventures in military

"Rose of York" : the Princess with her parents in front of the American Flying Fortress she had just christened.

An incident described at length in many letters mailed home to the United States : the Princess greets the crew of her Flying Fortress.

history, would welcome a sight of the Princess before they went, a thought amply proved right by the great welcome Elizabeth received wherever she went. As "D-Day" approached, the King spent more and more of his time away visiting concentration areas, making last inspections of divisions, brigades, and regiments, paying God-speed visits to the ships of his Navy, touring the R.A.F. stations where the preliminary operations were already begun, conferring with Montgomery and his other commanders in their secret advance headquarters. On most of these missions, the King went alone. The rules of secrecy were too strict to allow the slightest relaxation in favour of any civilian, even the King's daughter. But on some, where not quite the same conditions prevailed, the Queen and the Princess went with the King, to the great satisfaction of the troops concerned.

One such trip took her in the Royal train to two secret encampments, where she spent two full and exciting days with the King and Queen watching battle practice by picked shock troops and armoured formations. Another memorable occasion was when she and her mother were the only non-Service spectators to witness the most dramatic pre-battle rehearsal of all time, the final practice parachute jumps and glider landings by the Airborne Division, the very tip of the spearhead of the Allied invasion. In all the long panorama of great occasions, occasions of State, occasions of national mourning or

Ready for the road. Princess Elizabeth poses for a photograph in her smartly-cut ATS uniform before taking the wheel of an Army ambulance. Note her medal ribbons

Photograph: Crown Copyright Reserved

Just before her second big launch : the Princess concentrates as she prepares to christen the great aircraft carrier, H.M.S. Eagle.

rejoicing, occasions on which she has seen, or has herself taken part in, the making of history, none can be more vivid or more enduring in the Princess's memory than that she saw in the gleaming sunshine of a summer's day in Wiltshire in the year 1944.

Netheravon Station of the R.A.F., set in wide Salisbury Plain, was, as many local folk well knew, the training headquarters for some of our crack airborne troops as they prepared for the invasion of France in 1944. But on a fine May morning in that year, when a small procession of cars, one of them flying the miniature Royal Standard, drove up to the station headquarters, neither the Queen nor Princess Elizabeth, who were accompanying the King, knew exactly what the aerodrome was, or exactly what it was they were to see. The presence of Air Chief Marshal Sir Trafford Leigh-Mallory, Commander-in-Chief of the Allied Invasion Air Forces, and of Lieutenant-General "Boy" Browning, Commander of the Airborne Troops, invested the occasion with more than the ordinary importance of a routine visit, and there was a general feeling of expectancy in the air as the King, in the R.A.F. uniform which he wears so well, stepped out of the car followed by the Queen and the Princess. Only the top ranking officers, who knew very well what it was all about, were aware in advance that the Princess was coming with her parents. Others, from wing commanders and colonels to humble "erks" and privates, were taken by surprise when they saw her, and tried to guess what significance was to be read into her presence.

The Royal party spent the entire day with the R.A.F. men and their comrades of the Airborne Forces at Netheravon and nearby Bulford, inspecting airborne units, examining paratroopers' equipment, and watching a big display of formation dropping by several hundred paratroops. To Princess Elizabeth, it was fascinating. She asked a hundred quiet questions as officers showed her the miniature motor-cycles, the collapsible cycles, the light guns and even the small tanks which the glider men and paratroops took with them into the air.

Up in the control tower of the station, with the King and Queen, the Air Chief Marshal, and General Browning, the Princess looked out through the observation windows at a blue, empty sky. Suddenly, with no warning, the great shape of a Horsa glider came into view, followed by another, and another, and another, till the sky, empty no longer, seemed filled with the strange, sinister craft, making their noiseless way through the

Safely away : Princess Elizabeth watches H.M.S. Eagle take the water. Beside her is her father's First Sea Lord, Admiral of the Fleet Sir Andrew (now Lord) Cunningham.

air as if by magic. The first glider put down perfectly, stopped only a few yards from the Royal watchers. Close on its heels the second craft swooped down, and in a matter of minutes, the sky was empty again, the big airfield jammed with gliders, their wingtips almost touching, lined up nose to tail in long rows like so many motor-cars in a crowded park at a Cup Final.

Princess Elizabeth watched it all in silent amazement, as well she might, for nothing quite like it had ever been seen before by serviceman or civilian. It was the most astounding demonstration of mastery over the air, of precision and discipline in handling motorless planes that could be imagined. The men in the planes had bent the winds to their will like so many gods. Even as a peaceful display of gliding, it would have ranked as a wonder: the consciousness that all this was but a rehearsal for the real thing, when the pilots would have darkness and enemy gunfire to contend with besides the elements, made it all the more impressive. There was no speech from the King, no long panegyric for these men who rode the winds so masterfully on his business. That is not our English way. But the King's few quiet words of congratulation, uttered in conversational tones to the two commanders at his side, and underlined by the Queen, brought faint smiles of satisfaction and pleasure to the faces of Leigh-Mallory and Browning. They had been watching every move with careful attention and critical eyes, for on the success of this last practice landing depended the success of the landing in a few days time in France, and on that, in turn, might well depend the success or failure of the entire expedition. Now they knew that, as far as training and skill could prevail, success was assured. The rest they were content to leave in the hands of fate, and it was a very cheerful party indeed that sat down to tea after the landing.

Almost as impressive as the glider demonstration was the sight the Princess had seen earlier in the day, when several hundred paratroops dropped in accurate formation, their vari-coloured parachutes blossoming in a sudden widespread rash across the sky, floating lazily in slow peace to earth, where the men, stripping off their harness with practised speed, rushed in ordered haste to form their battle units, ready for action a few seconds after touching the ground.

Another outstanding day for the Princess was when, some time later, again accompanying her father and mother, she made a tour of four big stations of the Royal Canadian Air Force. It was an outstanding day for the R.C.A.F. as well, the first time the King had devoted a whole day to his Canadian Air Force, and the first time the Princess had visited Canadian "territory". Standing under the great wings of a dozen four-engined Halifax bombers in a hangar, the Princess watched her father decorating officers and men of the R.C.A.F. for their achievements in the D-day operations, the bombing of Caen, and in other notable air attacks. Over one hundred and fifty men from all parts of the Dominion, of all ranks from the Air Commodore from Ottawa, who headed the list, to humble aircraftsmen, received awards during the day, the names of their homes, towns and provinces, Moose Jaw, Medicine Hat, Winnipeg, Manitoba, Ontario, and so on, conjuring up a very real picture of the vast Dominion in the mind of the attentive Princess. There were lively touches in the day's programme, too, as when the Princess with her parents, went into the "Lion's Den"—to find the fearsome name merely indicated the crew room of the Lion Squadron: or when the King presented the squadron badge to the "Moose" Squadron, and the Princess saw the squadron motto, "Beware the Moose" emblazoned beneath it in Red Indian characters. Half seriously, and half laughing the Princess listened to a long discussion between the King and a young Flight-Lieutenant from Ontario about the debatable question of gremlins, those queer denizens of the upper air alleged to board aircraft at various times with friendly or evil intent. Paintings of an astonishing variety of gremlins decorated the walls of the squadron room, and the man from Ontario declared he had several times had such visitors aboard his plane, adding, with pretended seriousness, that they usually chose 3,000 feet as the height to join the aircraft.

The King, who dearly loves joking such as this, took up the tale, and told the Flight-Lieutenant of his own experiences with the gremlins, one of whom, he said, they thought they had heard on board the Royal aeroplane, when he was returning from Italy a week or two earlier. "But I told him to be quiet, and we heard no more," the King added, with a half-smile that left his hearer momentarily uncertain whether he was a subscriber to the gremlin theory or not, to the delight of the Princess, who had followed all the conversation with close interest.

This was not the Princess's only experience of air stations at invasion tension. A two-day tour of R.A.F. stations and U.S.A.A.F. stations which she carried out again with the King and Queen, a month after the first landings in Normandy, has a special place in her war memories. It was the first time she had been amongst the friendly informality of the American airmen: and it was the first—and up to now the only—occasion on which she has christened an aircraft. The tour started off in mild enough fashion, with a series of visits to R.A.F. stations where the King held several investitures in the hangars. After a night in the Royal train, the Princess drove next morning with her parents to one of the big Flying Fortress stations of the Eighth Air Force, where the Stars and Stripes flying over the buildings, the unfamiliar uniforms, the new words of command, the different method of presenting arms, helped to build up a delightful impression of freshness and novelty.

It was smiling, diminutive General "Jimmy" Doolittle, Commander of the Eighth Air Force, and hero of the first American bombing attack on Tokio, who had the pleasant task of showing the Royal visitors round the four stations they visited. At the first, the Princess had an unexpected thrill when she saw dozens of Flying Forts touching down after a highly successful raid on the German flying-bomb sites on the Pas de Calais. Then, in the middle of a crowd of cheering G.I.s, she stood with the King and Queen and General Doolittle, watching more massive formations of Forts pass overhead on their way to deliver a fresh attack on the same target. It was the boisterous informality of the G.I.s and their vociferous welcome that struck Princess Elizabeth most, in contrast to the no less eager, but more restrained and more quietly expressed welcome she was used to seeing at R.A.F. stations. And there were the cameras. Besides the large contingent of Press and Army photographers from London, half the officers and a third of the enlisted men on each station seemed to have a camera and an ambition to get a close-up of the Princess and her parents. Overwhelming as this must have been, the King and Queen, with the Princess standing a little in the rear, took it all without demur, with the result that—if only they came out—to-day more amateur snapshots of the British Sovereign, his consort and his heiress, must grace good republican homes in the United States than are to be found in loyal monarchist homes in many nations of the British Empire.

The American airmen scored another friendly victory that day over their comrades of the Royal Air Force and the Royal Canadian Air Force alike, a victory that was a tribute to American initiative and to the democratic organisation of the U.S. Army and its Air Force. Some weeks before, when rumour said that a Royal visit was to be expected, Master Sergeant J. Gregory, hailing from Salt Lake City, Utah, had a bright idea. "Let's ask for Princess Elizabeth to name our bomber after her," said he. The wheels of officialdom began to revolve, the sergeant's idea went up through the military hierarchy till it was put before the King, who approved, with the sole proviso that the aircraft should be named not Princess Elizabeth, but "Rose of York" to maintain the rule that Royal family names are only given to ships in the Royal Navy. (*Queen Elizabeth* and *Queen Mary*, the Atlantic liners, are the only exceptions.) So it came about that it was an

" Well away ! " : the Princess smiles as, with Admiral of the Fleet Lord Cunningham at her side, she sees the great battleship Vanguard slip down the ways after she has launched her.

Immediately after the launch : Princess Elizabeth sees the tugs take charge of H.M.S. Vanguard as she enters the Clyde.

American, and not a British or a Canadian aircraft which the Princess christened, and not even a new plane at that, for Rose of York had accomplished thirteen missions, the first of them to Berlin, before the "christening day" arrived. Had a similiar idea been put forward first by the R.A.F. or the R.C.A.F., the same permission would most probably have been forthcoming: but neither of the King's own services ventured to make the suggestion.

Officers and G.I.s, air crews and ground staffs, stood in a semi-circle round the Princess as she faced the silver-shining aircraft, with its thirteen tell-tale bombs on the fuselage, below the inscription "Rose of York" newly painted on the nose. Confidently and with little trace of nerves, Princess Elizabeth smashed a bottle of British cider against the nose of the bomber, and named it. Now it was the King and Queen who stood behind, watching their daughter take the centre of the stage. So charmingly did the Princess perform the little ceremony that a vote on that station would have nominated her the most popular person alive! When she had named "her" aircraft, the Princess shook hands with all ten members of the Fortress crew, and wished them good luck and success on all future missions. The plane ended its career in March 1945, when it failed to return from a raid on Berlin.

Up to November 1944, the Princess had not figured in any big wartime naval occasion: but the Royal Navy was rewarded for its patience when the King sent his daughter to launch the mightiest battleship yet built, H.M.S. *Vanguard*, the ship he later chose to carry the Royal family on their first post-war Empire visit to South Africa.

It was the Princess's first public engagement of national importance, and though war-time security perforce robbed the occasion of some of its interest, since neither the locality of the launch nor the name of the ship could be published, the nation as a whole recognised it as marking the real entry of the heiress to the throne into national life. Other appear-ances the Princess had made in public were all of a comparatively minor nature: this time she was to carry out a ceremony of major character, one which might well cause much older and more experienced people to pause. Princess Elizabeth prepared for the ordeal with her usual thoroughness and composure. She read and rehearsed the speech she was to make again and again until she was word perfect. She asked the King and Queen, and all the senior naval officers she could find, all they could tell her about launches and what went on at them.

Vanguard was built in Messrs. John Brown's yard at Clydebank, so that St. Andrew's Day was particularly appropriate for her launch. The night before, Princess Elizabeth, accompanied by her lady-in-waiting and one naval officer from her father's staff, set off on the all-night train journey to Glasgow. Station officials who saw her off at Euston, and those who received her at the end of the journey, all remarked on her composure and calm. But inwardly, Princess Elizabeth was not quite so calm. When a member of the party remarked on the cold—for it was a raw November morning, with a chill breeze blowing up the Clyde—the Princess, with much feeling in her tone, replied, "I'm much too nervous to feel the cold!" Yet, when she walked through the crowds of cheering Clydesiders who had built the great warship, there was not a sign of nerves to ruffle her outward composure. She walked under the huge steel hull, more than a little awed by the gargantuan size of even the holding chains and cables which would pull up the ship when she took the water. No one of imagination can ever fail to be thrilled by the

Princess Elizabeth with the Navy: a Portsmouth inspection

launch of a big ship. On the stocks, she seems so much dead weight, an almost immovable, certainly lifeless, mass of steel. Then, as she, slowly at first, with gathering momentum, takes the water, the ship becomes alive, the inert steel mass is transformed into an entity of grace and power and beauty.

Princess Elizabeth had heard all that long before she took her place on the flag-draped launching platform, surrounded by her father's Admirals and Captains, with the First Lord of the Admiralty, Mr. A. V. Alexander, the First Sea Lord, Admiral of the Fleet Sir Andrew Cunningham (now Lord Cunningham of Hyndhope), and Lord Aberconway, chairman of the shipbuilders, at her side. With a pair of silver scissors, she cut a tape, a bottle of Empire wine smashed against the tall bows, and, in a clear firm voice that showed no trace of the nervous strain which she must have been feeling, she said "I name this ship the *Vanguard*. May God bless this ship and all who serve in her." To the accompaniment of a roar of full-throated lusty Scots cheering, she pressed a button to set the electric launching gear in motion, and looked up expectantly at the grey stem towering above her, waiting for the miracle of ship-birth to happen.

But nothing did happen. The cheers died away. For a brief moment that seemed to stretch out in time, the ship stayed stationary. The Princess stood motionless, in a silence that was complete. Then, almost imperceptibly, the ship began to move on the stocks, the tension was over, the silence shattered by louder cheers than ever. Her face flushed with excitement and pleasure, Princess Elizabeth turned to Lord Aberconway as if to ask him if she had done her part. He shook her hand, warmly congratulating her, while the tugs took charge of the big ship. Delightedly, the Princess gazed down on the crowds of workmen and women below her, and waved her grey gloved hand to them in a spontaneous gesture that reminded everyone instantly of the Queen.

When at the luncheon which followed, Lord Aberconway presented her with a magnificent diamond brooch, shaped as the Rose of England, to be a souvenir of the occasion, the Princess said "This will always serve to remind me that the first important public duty I ever undertook was a naval occasion." They were simple words, simply spoken, but they hit exactly the right note. Over the shipyard, the Princess's personal standard, with its white cadency label, made for her by the Royal Navy, flew for the first time: and in the hearts of the men and women, of high rank or low, who had watched her ease of manner, her friendliness, and her charm, she took her place for the first time as Princess Charming.

No greater success could possibly have been won, no one could have been more happy than the King and Queen when they heard, as they took pains that they should hear, full reports of how the Princess had fared. It was more than a personal triumph for the young Princess: it was the happiest of auguries for the future.

Since then, the Princess has launched two more ships, one the great aircraft carrier, H.M.S. *Eagle*, built by Messrs. Harland and Wolff at Belfast, the other a much humbler vessel of the merchant navy, the oil tanker *British Princess*, built in the Deptford yard on Wearside, which she launched as a special if tardy token of the nation's recognition of the tanker crews without whose devoted, often unrecognised service, as the Princess said, no ship of the Royal Navy could have moved. On both occasions, she acquitted herself with equal ease and success: and at both launches she was given a brooch as a souvenir, a diamond eagle at Belfast, a diamond and sapphire flower brooch at Sunderland.

Those launches were performed after the war had ended. While Japan was still fighting, the Princess went on two other naval occasions with the King and Queen, when the King went to bid Godspeed and good luck to the battleship *King George V*, before she sailed from Greenock to be Admiral Fraser's flagship in the Pacific, and again when the King went with similar purpose aboard the aircraft *Indefatigable* at Portsmouth. In *K.G.*5, the Princess, with her sister Margaret, went exploring the big triple fourteen inch gun turrets, escorted by a delighted gunnery officer and an officer of Marines. Then she saw ammunition being taken aboard, stepping nimbly out of the way as straining ratings and marines pushed and heaved at the trolleys carrying the huge, heavy projectiles. It was another new experience for her, and one, again, which no King's daughter had ever had before her.

A sequel to the *Vanguard* launch came eighteen months later, when the Princess went north again, this time to Greenock, where the battleship lay, newly commissioned. Aboard *Vanguard*, she attended the "commissioning service" with its ancient bidding prayers, said by the captain and crew, and dating back to the sixteenth century and the ships of that other Elizabeth who was Queen. She attended, too, the dedication of the ship's chapel to St. Andrew of Scotland. Before she said good-bye to *Vanguard* for the second time, Captain W. G. Agnew, her commander, took her over those parts of the ship which would be the floating home for herself, her sister, and their parents on their voyage to South Africa, then nine months ahead.

CHAPTER TWELVE

What To-morrow May Hold

THE PRINCESS'S FUTURE

IN the forefront of any consideration of the future of Princess Elizabeth is, inevitably, the question of her marriage. On this topic much has been written, and more, much more, talked, in the past two years. Her name has been the central theme in the gossip of tea-parties in Mayfair, in the suburbs of London, in provincial cities, in the Dominions, and in the United States as well, as aged ladies have hunted through Debrett, Kelly's, and the Almanach de Gotha tracing the ancestry and family status of the latest young man mentioned as a potential suitor. At least half a dozen young peers or sons of peers, who are numbered among Princess Elizabeth's wide circle of friends, have had the unpleasant spotlight of gossip focused on them in this way for no reason more than that they have been seen two or three times in the Princess's company. Several foreign Royalties, some eligible, some definitely not eligible, have been added from time to time to the gossips' list, regardless of the fact that some of the young Princelings concerned have never met or seen the Princess.

All this is, naturally, distasteful in the extreme to Princess Elizabeth, and to the King and Queen as well. But the question of her marriage is of such outstanding importance and interest to the Empire at large that there can be no means of stopping speculation. In the United States, too, where the young and attractive heiress to the greatest throne in the world is regarded with much romantic interest, the merest breath of a suggestion that the Princess is showing favour to one young man more than the others, at once starts a flood of newspaper stories. The first speculations about a marriage for the Princess appeared when she was only four years old. One periodical then set out a list of eight candidates whom it deemed possible as future suitors.

Since then, all sorts of names, probable and improbable, have been added by rumour to swell the lists. More than one of the young men concerned have married. They and their wives are still on the same terms of friendship with the Princess as before, for what the rumour-mongers and gossip-makers seem unable to grasp is that Princess Elizabeth, just like any other young woman of her age to-day, has a great many friends of both sexes, who are friends, and not more than friends. When she began to go out in the evenings to theatres and dances, rumours redoubled, and the name of each of her dancing partners was carefully noted—a practice which only led to the confusion of the gossips, since there were so many of them, and none seemed to occur with any significant frequency.

The plain fact is that up to the present, there is, and has been, no basis whatever for any of these rumours, which serve no good purpose, but merely tend to distress the Princess, and make her all the more determined to insist that her right to some privacy in her own life shall be respected, all the more rightly intolerant of any attempts to intrude upon it. Whether she will marry, when she will marry, whom she may marry, are matters on which she may justly claim the right of a twentieth century Princess to decide for

With her grandmother: a specially posed picture on her eighteenth birthday, when Queen Mary visited her at Windsor.

herself when the time comes: and until that time, wild guesses and idle ill-informed conjectures about matrimony form the one—and almost the only—feature of her position which she regards with resentment.

When Albert Edward, Prince of Wales, afterwards King Edward VII, was twenty years old, a list of suitable Princesses from whom he might choose his bride was drawn up. It was a very short list, and how far the Prince would have been allowed a free choice even from it is problematical, for on the sage advice of "Uncle Leopold"—King Leopold I of the Belgians—it was with the lively Princess Alexandra of Denmark that the first meeting was arranged for him. Arrangements, quite elaborate arrangements, were made

The Day of the Crowns: a family group after the Coronation ceremony.

for the two to meet at one of the lesser German courts, and even more care was taken to give the meeting an outward appearance of casualness. In spite of all these cumbersome formalities, the two took to each other, the engagement was announced a few months later, and "Uncle Leopold" could sit back and smile at having successfully arranged yet another marriage between the Royal families of Europe.

Whatever else is uncertain, it is true and sure that no such arranged match has ever been contemplated for Princess Elizabeth. There is certainly no "Uncle Leopold" to-day to offer advice, and if there were it would not be wanted. The marriage of the Duke of York with Lady Elizabeth Bowes-Lyon was a love match. No fetters were put by King George V on his second son's choice of a bride. Since then the world's views have broadened rather than narrowed, until to-day the very hint that constraint might be put on a young girl to marry against her will, be she Princess or no, is unthinkable. No such thought has ever entered the mind of the King or Queen about Princess Elizabeth.

But nevertheless, there are certain restrictions and limitations which must govern the Princess's choice, restrictions imposed not by the Royal family in the way the once-imperious House of Hohenzollern used to govern the alliance of its cadets, but by the British Parliament. Under the terms of the Act "for Declaring the Rights and Liberties of the Subject, and settling the succession of the Crown," (I William and Mary, C.2) commonly known as the Bill of Rights, succession to the crown is expressly barred from all persons holding communion with the Church of Rome or "marrying a Papist". So rigorous are the terms of that still-binding Act that it is laid down that in such a case, the

After standing "Kuom" or Godmother to the infant Crown Prince of Jugo-Slavia at Westminster Abbey. The Princess holds her hat as she waits for the Royal car.

people are absolved of their allegiance, and the Crown descends to "such person or persons being Protestants as should have inherited and enjoyed the same, in case the said person or persons so reconciled, holding communion, or professing (the Church of Rome) or marrying, as aforesaid, were naturally dead."

Further limitations are imposed by the Royal Marriages Act (12 Geo. III, C. II) passed in 1772, in consequence of the marriages of the Dukes of Cumberland and Gloucester. It enacts that "No descendant of his late Majesty George II (other than the issue of Princesses who have married or who may marry into foreign families) shall be capable of contracting matrimony without the previous consent of His Majesty, his heirs and successors, signified under the Great Seal. But in case any descendant of George II, being above twenty-five years old, shall persist to contract a marriage disapproved of by His Majesty, such descendant, after giving twelve months notice to the Privy Council, may contract such marriage, and the same may be duly solemnised, without the consent of His Majesty, his heirs and successors, and shall be good except both Houses of Parliament shall declare their disapprobation thereto."

The Act gives the Sovereign of the day a very considerable, though not absolute, power over the marriages of all those in direct sucession to the Crown. In effect, it means that the King's consent must be declared in Council before any such marriage can take place.

The earlier Act limits absolutely the choice of Princess Elizabeth, or anyone else in the line of succession, to non-Catholics.

But beyond those constitutional restrictions, there is no other limit or bar on the score of birth or nationality on whom a British Princess may marry. No longer must she

With Australian ex-prisoners of war who were captured at Tobruk. Princess Elizabeth talks to a nursing commandant from Sydney at a Buckingham Palace party.

contemplate marriage with one inside the prescribed golden circle of those of Royal blood or be content not to marry at all. Princess Elizabeth's mother was a commoner when she married the then Duke of York, for the "lady" in her title as an Earl's daughter was a courtesy title only, conferring no right in the peerage, yet there have been few, if any, Queen Consorts in our history who have carried out their duties with more regal dignity and grace, or won a higher place in the hearts of the people.

There is, as yet, no precedent for a marriage between a member of the Royal house and a citizen of one of the Dominions, but there is no reason whatever why such a match might not be made. Under the Statute of Westminster the King is King equally of each of his Dominions, as he is King of the United Kingdom, and the subjects of the King of Canada, for example, enjoy therefore exactly the same equal rights, have the same equal legal status as the English or Scots subjects of the same monarch. If there is no ban on a Royal marriage with an English commoner, neither, then, can there be any ban on one with a commoner from the Dominions. Foreign marriages have, of a certainty, been frequent in days gone by, so, again, there is nothing in law to stop the Princess marrying a national of any other country, from Denmark to the United States. Whoever she may marry would take no actual share in the government of the United Kingdom or the

Dominions or the rest of the Empire, if the Princess came to the Throne, any more than Her Majesty the Queen does to-day. She is Queen Consort to King George VI. The Princess would be Queen Regnant, and her husband would probably—though not necessarily—be given Royal rank as a Prince Consort.

Some idea of the peculiar circumstances surrounding such a position may be gained from the terms of a note written by Queen Victoria's beloved Albert, after ten years experience as Prince Consort.

"Whilst a female Sovereign has a great many disadvantages," wrote that observant, studious, and sagacious Prince, "in comparison with a King, yet, if she is married, and her husband understands and does his duty, her position, on the other hand, has its many compensating advantages, and, in the long run, will be found even to be stronger than that of a male sovereign. But this requires that the husband should entirely sink his own *individual* existence in that of his wife: that he should aim at no power by himself or for himself: should shun all contention, assume no separate responsibility before the public but make his position entirely a part of hers: fill up every gap which, as a woman, she would naturally leave in the exercise of her regal functions: continually and anxiously watch every part of public business, in order to be able to advise and assist her at any moment in any of the multifarious and difficult questions or duties brought before her, sometimes international, sometimes political, social or personal."

It sounds a formidable list!

Marriage, however interesting a topic, however important in its consequences, is by no means the only aspect of Princess Elizabeth's future to be considered. The Royal visit to South Africa, planned as the first Empire tour of post-war days, was also conceived, partly at the suggestion of General Smuts, as a first introduction of the Princess to the Empire, and of the Empire to the Princess. Each of the other Dominions has made known to the King the desire of its people to see the heiress to the throne, and there is good hope that, with her parents, or alone, Princess Elizabeth will, in the next few years, make several overseas visits to various parts of the Empire. Since King Edward VII made his first visit to Canada and the United States when Prince of Wales—he travelled "incognito" as Baron Renfrew—such visits have, to an increasing degree, come to be regarded as an essential part of the education and training of those in close succession to the throne. To-day when wireless and air travel have so shrunk the world's distances, they must be more, and not less, important steps in the upbringing of one who must, one day, be prepared to have problems and questions from all parts of the Empire brought to her, and be able to see them all in relation to each other and to the whole. Princess Elizabeth herself, in her talks with various Dominion statesmen whom she has met on their visits to this country, has made no secret of her own keen desire to see as much as she can of the Empire which she already knows so well from reading and hearsay. No "master plan" for a succession of visits has been made, nor is such a scheme in contemplation. The claims of each Dominion will be weighed, with other relevant circumstances, as the case arises. After South Africa, Canada would seem to have the prior claim, as the oldest of the Dominions. But Canada received the first Royal visit of the reign, in 1939, and, should Princess Elizabeth's next tour be again one with the King and Queen, it is likely that one of the other Dominions would be chosen. All that is certain is that the Princess is as eager to see the Empire as the Empire is to see the Princess: and both sooner or later will have their wishes fulfilled.

Meanwhile, at home, the course of the Princess's life is most likely to continue on its present lines. Gradually she will take an increasing share of more important public duties. Less and less of her time will be left to her for her own enjoyment as a private individual. But she will continue to enjoy herself none the less, for it is one of the secrets of Princess Elizabeth's happiness that she takes an interest in everything. One of the older members of the Royal family was discoursing for a long time to the Princess, a few years ago, on Queen Victoria and her children who had been the dominant figures of her own childhood's world. Abruptly, the elder Royalty broke off with the remark, "All this must be very dull for you. Of course you never knew any of these people." "N t at all," replied the Princess. "It is most interesting. To me it's like history coming to li?

That ability to see the interesting side of even the dullest functions has already stood the Princess in good stead. It will be of increasing value to her as the years pass, an indispensable adjunct in her equipment for the life of a twentieth-century Princess and future Queen.